Multiple Intelligences

Structures & Activities

by Laurie Kagan

Kagan Publishing
981 Calle Amanecer
San Clemente, CA 92673
1 (800) 933-2667
www.KaganOnline.com

ISBN: 978-1-879097-46-9

Table of Contents

Introduction 4
The Eight Intelligences
Word Smart 8
Logic/Math Smart 10
Art/Space Smart 12
Music Smart 14
Body Smart 16
Nature Smart 18
People Smart 20
Self Smart 22
Top 10 Reasons to Care About Multiple Intelligences 24
Kagan's Multiple Intelligences Structures 25
Blind Sequencing Structure 26
Goldilocks 28
The Napping House 31
Crazy Quilt 36
Our School 38
Draw A Gambit 40
Perfect Praisers 42
Paraphrase Gambits 44
Disagree Gambits 45
What Do U Think? 48
Coaching Gambits 50
Requesting Explanation 51
Draw What I Write 52
Clown Face Painter 54
Bear and Giraffe 56
Pirate's Treasure 59
Shapes 62
John's Route 64
Rectangles 66
Fan-N-Pick 68
Bee Honest 70
The Giving Tree 74
Shining Stars 76
Book Reports 78
The Question Box 82
Express Yourself 84
Trading Places 85
Describe U'rself 86
Space 88

Guided Imagery 90
The Underground Railroad 93
A Miracle in Nature 96
Hearty Voyage 98
An Enjoyable Day 100
Someone Special 101
My Room 102
Circus 104
Jigsaw Problem-Solving 106
The Lost Clown 108
The Wise Old Owl 113
Peter Penguin's Problems 118
Around the World 124
Skiing Lake Tahoe 127
Historical Moments 129
Farmer John's Garden 136
Barnyard Animals 142
Logic Line-Ups 146
Rainforest Logic 148
Our Team 153
The Clown's Crayons 158
Pocket Change 163
Sunday Drive 168
Lyrical Lessons 174
School Days
It's Time 176
What Makes You Angry? 177
School is Cool 178
Language Arts
Samuel Clemens 179
Laura Ingalls 180
AEIOU 181
Mathematics
Three's Table 182
The Gallon Table 183
When The Signs Come Marching In 184
Math Music 187
Science
Louis Pasteur 188
Jacques Cousteau 189
Water Cycle 190
Solar System 191
The Seasons 192

Social Studies
Christopher Columbus . . . 193
Colonial Times . . . 194
Seeking Freedom . . . 195
Christopher Columbus . . . 196
Ben Franklin . . . 197
Independence . . . 198
Thomas Jefferson . . . 199
Pocahontas . . . 200
Gold Rush . . . 201
Wild, Wild West . . . 202
Pony Express . . . 203
Abraham Lincoln . . . 204
From Our View . . . 205
Flappers . . . 206
Celebrate History . . . 207
Same-Different . . . 209
Recording Sheet . . . 210
Take A Good Look Recording Sheet . . . 211
Money Matters . . . 212
Geo-Movers . . . 213
Butterfly/Moth Pictures . . . 214
Butterfly/Moth Stories . . . 216
Fish Bowl . . . 218
Our Town . . . 220
Dino Days . . . 222
Captain Coop Cereal . . . 224
Welcome Home . . . 226
The Train . . . 228
Sequencing . . . 230
Human Happenings . . . 232
The Great Candybar Heist . . . 233
It Got Away . . . 234
The Confused Pledge of Allegiance . . . 236
Three Wise Owls . . . 238
Space . . . 239
Pigs in a Blanket . . . 243
Answers . . . 248
Blind Sequencing Section . . . 250
Jigsaw Problem-Solving Section . . . 254
Logic Line-Ups Section . . . 260
Same-Different Section . . . 265
Resources . . . 272

Introduction

Howard Gardner's writings point out that kids are smart in many ways. When I read Gardner's work it seemed to me so natural that I wondered why more of us had not thought about intelligence in that way.

As teachers, we know each student is born with a unique intelligence profile. Each of us, in fact, is a combination of different intelligences and that combination defines our individuality. Every human being is special. As teachers, we need to recognize and nurture all the varied human intelligences and the unique ways they combine in each student.

This book presents a new approach to implementing Gardner's theory of Multiple Intelligences. Rather than planning MI lessons or creating MI learning centers or assessing individual students, it uses Kagan's structural approach. In the structural approach, teachers engage and develop the intelligences by using simple instructional strategies called structures. The beauty of these structures is that they can be used as part of almost any lesson, without special planning or changes in the curriculum.

In this book, you will find activities based on 10 carefully selected Kagan structures. You will receive step-by-step instructions on how to use each structure and a multitude of activities.

This book is designed for busy classroom teachers who are looking for ready-made activities. Teaching is hard work. Through this book I have tried to make your job easier by creating exciting lessons and activities. The book is packed with tons of blacklines, things to make, and cards to manipulate. The activities are planned around everyday classroom themes and will be a welcome addition for almost any teacher. Each blackline is ready to use, designed to engage and develop one or more of the intelligences.

No activity engages only one intelligence, and no structure develops only one intelligence. When students are working in a structure, we see the intelligences interacting. Some activities, though, are designed to stimulate primarily some intelligences, other activities other intelligences. Because as a collection the activities stretch all of the intelligences, through the activities every student works sometimes in areas which need improvement, and sometimes in areas of strength.

This book has two main goals. One purpose is to provide you with practical, hands-on activities you can use tomorrow to increase student engagement, learning, thinking, and intelligences.

The second purpose is to provide you with support in implementing Kagan structures. The hope is that once you have tried some of the activities in this book and learned the steps of the multiple intelligences structures, you will go on to use the structures on a regular basis with any content you are teaching. If so, you will be creating a multiple intelligences classroom. My hope is that this book helps open the doors to discovery of the power and fun in the easy-to-use Kagan structures.

For the teacher familiar with Kagan structures, this book will be a welcome storehouse of ready-made, innovative multiple intelligences activities. This book will bring MI to life in your classroom.

For the teacher new to Kagan structures, this book, hopefully, will be the first step as you embark on a journey of adventure and exploration. The structural approach empowers us to deliver any content in more varied, engaging, and impactive ways. The structures allow us to stimulate the range of intelligences without deviating from our regular curriculum. In the process all students become involved and develop more of their intelligences.

One of the powerful outcomes of using the structures to put multiple intelligences theory into practice is that we begin to look at our students through a new set of glasses. A student who looks rather dull when taught with only verbal instructional methods suddenly appears brilliant when taught with visual/spatial structures.

Another student who performs very poorly when working only alone, suddenly becomes a leader and achiever when allowed to work in an interpersonal/social structure. When we begin using a range of structures to stimulate the range of intelligences, we are surprised and delighted to discover hidden potential in our students.

Another powerful outcome of using the structures is that our role changes. Instead of the "sage on the stage" we become the "guide on the side." As we become a facilitator, guiding, coaching, encouraging students along their own journey of discovery, we rediscover joy in teaching. Because the students are so engaged in learning, we are free to enjoy the process. We make better contact with the students, get to know and like them better, and feel better about ourselves.

Yet another positive outcome of the structural approach is the shift from MI lesson planning to the ongoing use of MI structures. If we spend a night planning a great MI lesson and deliver it perfectly the next day, the students have had the benefit of one great MI lesson. If instead we learn the MI structures, we make every lesson an MI lesson. Through the structures we make multiple intelligences part of every lesson.

Students, too, are transformed by the structures. The classroom-tested activities in this book make learning fun and engaging for all students. Students, regardless of their unique pattern of intelligences, will have a greater opportunity to fulfill their potential. In the process they

discover within themselves a new eagerness to learn and new abilities and strengths.

When we use a range of structures to engage the range of intelligences, students actually get smarter. They feel more competent and better about themselves. They become better prepared to work in the world which will unfold over the course of the 21st century, a world we can only dimly imagine, but a world in which students who can use the range of intelligences will have an advantage.

Our world is growing more complex and interdependent. The students of today who regularly engage the range of intelligences will have an advantage in the world of tomorrow in which we will use technology to integrate logic, words, music, art, nature, and social interaction.

How To Use This Book

There is no one right way to use this book. You may decide to take one structure and try to master it, first using the activities in the book and later using the structure to design new activities based on your own content. Or you may jump around, trying various activities that catch your fancy or correspond to your curriculum. Sequential or random, either style will find in the book plenty to work with.

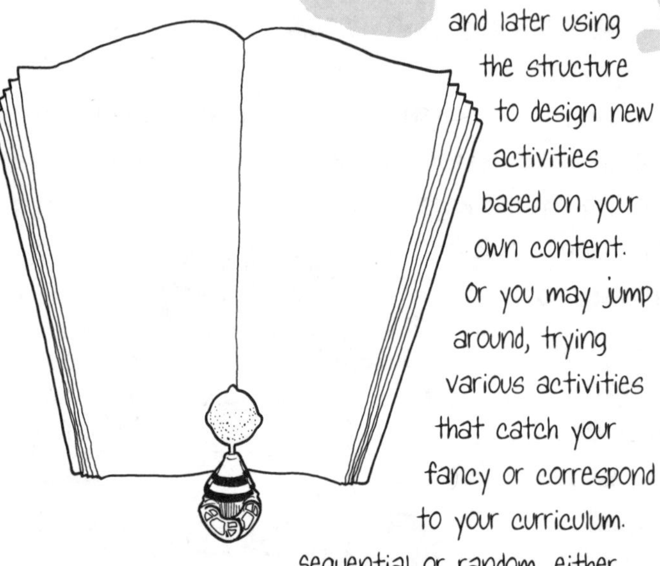

Below are some ideas to spin off from:

- Select an intelligence you would like to nurture, an intelligence students are having difficulty with, and use structures and activities which engage that intelligence.
- Select an intelligence of strength for your classroom and use the structures to develop new facets of that intelligence - take your students to an even higher level.
- Select activities which correspond to your curriculum or the interests of your students.
- Master one structure at a time, not taking up a second structure until you can do the first one "in your sleep," with almost any content with little or no preparation.
- Use the activities for rainy days.
- Place the activities in your folder for substitute teachers. (When we are sick, it is the time we least want to be preparing lessons for a sub; use this book to have engaging activities ready-made).
- For activities involving manipulatives, pair up with a buddy-teacher to cut the prep time in half and to double the support.

Preparing Students for an Unknown Future

Our job as educators is to prepare students for their future, not our yesterdays. Their world will little resemble the world we grew up in. How can we best prepare them for their journey into the unknown? How can we know what best to teach?

The content we teach today soon will be outdated; our students will be working with information and technology we cannot now imagine.

What is the constant? The constant is intelligence. No matter what information our students will deal with, they will be more successful if they can think about that information in many ways - use multiple intelligences. So if we are not teaching in many ways, stimulating the range of intelligences, we are not preparing our students for their journey.

In preparing students for the future, we are drawn into new ways of teaching. The structures provide an easy way for us to engage and develop the range of intelligences, to prepare students for their journey into an unknown future.

With Appreciation

There are many people to whom I am grateful and want to express my appreciation. First to the thousands of teachers I have worked with and learned from throughout the years. Each of these interactions have helped me shape my understanding and added to the texture of this book.

Also, to my husband, Spencer Kagan, who has provided me with large doses of love and support. He has always stood by my side, encouraging me each step of the way. Without his support and invaluable advice, this book would not be a reality.

I acknowledge with thanks all the individuals who helped with the development and production of this book:

To Celso Rodgriguez who delightfully illustrated each activity. With a few strokes he made simple ideas come to life. His warm and whimsical style is a great guide for teachers and students alike. Celso's art showcases the best of the Kagan structures and the MI activities.

To Kristen Lange for all her time and attention to detail. She has taken scratchy, hand-drawn pages and converted them into teacher-friendly, ready-to-use resources.

To Miguel Kagan for his guidance and coordination of this book's production. With his meticulous editing, he gave so generously countless helpful suggestions which contribute to a more understandable text.

To Jeanne Murphy for her wise reading of the manuscript and her precision in editing.

To Todd Whitaker and Liz Warner for providing their musical insights and their input that helped clarify the Lyrical Lessons.

To all the staff at Kagan Publishing who have been supportive and patient.

I wish you wonderful experiences with these MI activities. I hope you enjoy the activities as much as I have enjoyed coming up with them!

Laurie Kagan

Word Smart

When students use their Verbal/Linguistic intelligence, they are being "Word Smart."

Students show they are word smart when they are good at reading, writing, speaking, and listening. They use language to express ideas, experiences, and images.

Being word smart includes enjoying reading, telling stories and jokes, and having a good vocabulary. Word smart also includes having a sensitivity to the order and meaning of words and also their sounds, rhythms, and inflections.

We show this intelligence as we write stories, poems, jokes, letters, and journals. We are also word smart when we show an interest in debates, storytellers, class discussions, and oral presentations.

People who put their word smarts to work include authors, poets, public speakers, attorneys, salespeople, actors/actresses, comedians, journalists, and politicians.

We are Word Smart when we:

- Learn through reading, writing, discussing
- Communicate effectively, orally and in writing
- Display a rich vocabulary
- Write clearly
- Spell easily
- Think in words, play with words
- Love to tell stories or jokes
- Enjoy poetry
- Communicate with colorful and descriptive phrases
- Play word games
- Like to put thoughts on paper in letters, journals, or creative writing
- Remember quotes and sayings

Logic/Math Smart

When students use their Logical/Mathematical intelligence, they are being "Math Smart."

Students show they are Logic/Math smart when they use numbers, symbols, computations, and when they quantify and sequence.

Being Logic/Math smart includes problem solving, inductive and deductive thinking, and recognizing abstract patterns.

Logic/Math smart also includes the ability to solve riddles, logic puzzles, and brain teasers. Logic smart students ask about how things work!

We show this intelligence as we find patterns and relationships among objects and numbers. We are Logic/Math smart also when we seek cause-effect relations and use abstract reasoning.

People who put their Logic/Math smarts to work include bankers, entrepreneurs, accountants, scientists, computer programmers, judges, mathematicians, and detectives.

We are Logic/Math Smart when we:

Logical Mathematical

1 2 3

- Think in numbers and symbols
- Make lists
- Classify and categorize objects
- Figure things out (such as how much to leave for a tip)
- Set priorities
- Decipher codes
- Find and create patterns
- Outline, organize, and sequence
- Play strategy games like chess and checkers
- Ask questions in a logical manner
- Solve problems
- Estimate and predict

Art/Space Smart

When students use their Visual/Spatial intelligence, they are being "Art/Space Smart."

Students show they are Art/Space smart when they think in, with, and about visual images.

Being Art/Space smart includes skill with the visual arts - painting and sculpting, and visual assembly - taking things apart and putting them together.

Art/Space smart also includes the ability to express oneself by drawing, painting, and creating models.

We show this intelligence as we have an eye for details, colors, line, shape, form, and space. We are Art/Space smart also when we "see" through visualization and imagination and learn well through guided imagery, and visual aids such as films, videos, posters, and diagrams.

People who put their Art/Space smarts to work include artists, navigators, painters, architects, sculptors, photographers, decorators, designers, florists, pilots, and navigators.

We are Art/Space Smart when we:

- Think in pictures and images
- Rotate figures mentally
- Orient our body in space
- Create three-dimensional models
- Maintain a sense of direction
- Imagine in vivid detail (visualize)
- Solve jigsaw problems
- Create visual/spatial representations of the world
- Produce and decode graphic information
- Arrange and decorate
- Paint, sketch, and draw
- Coordinate colors

Musical/Rhythmic

Music Smart

When students use their Musical/Rhythmic intelligence, they are being "Music Smart."

Students show they are Music Smart when they are sensitive to pitch, timbre, timing, tone, rhythm and sounds.

Being Music Smart includes sensitivity to vocal, instrumental, and environmental sounds. Music smart also includes the ability to express oneself through music and rhythm.

We show this intelligence as we play instruments, sing songs, read music, compose melodies and lyrics, and appreciate music. We are Music Smart also when we are whistling, humming, and tapping our hands and feet.

People who put their Music Smarts to work include musicians, composers, conductors, disc jockeys, instrument makers, singers, and music critics.

We are Music Smart when we:

- Enjoy listening to music
- Key in to sounds around us
- Sing, whistle, or hum while doing other things
- Collect CDs and tapes
- Keep time and recognize rhythm
- Play a musical instrument
- Read and write music
- Sing in key
- Understand the structure of music
- Recognize melodies, songs, and composers
- Identify musical instruments
- Make up songs to remember information

Body Smart

When students use their Bodily/Kinesthetic intelligence, they are being "Body Smart."

Students show they are Body Smart when they use their motor skills, use their hands and bodies to communicate, and unite body and mind to perfect physical performance.

Developing Body Smarts includes developing speed, strength, flexibility, agility, coordination, and endurance. Body Smart also includes the ability to express oneself through movements, gestures, and body language.

We show this intelligence as we enjoy physical activities such as dancing, athletics, acting, or "hands-on" activities like building and manipulating things. We are Body Smart also when we use the body in highly differentiated and skilled ways such as mime and acrobatics.

People who put their Body Smarts to work include athletes, surgeons, physical therapists, dancers, magicians, carpenters, jewelers, and gymnasts.

We are Body Smart when we:

- Move with grace and coordination
- Act and mimic
- Process information through bodily sensations
- Enjoy movement
- Use and understand gestures and body language
- Communicate information by modeling
- Touch people we talk to
- Appreciate athletic performances
- Learn through "hands-on" activities
- Play sports
- Dance and choreograph
- Benefit when movements are used to symbolize content

Naturalist

Nature Smart

When students use their Naturalist intelligence, they are being "Nature Smart."

Students show they are Nature Smart when they are keenly aware of the natural world around them.

Being Nature Smart includes discriminating natural items like animals, insects, birds, fish, rocks, minerals, stars, and plants. Nature Smart also extends to sensitivity to and interest in man-made objects which are part of our environment such as cars, types of sneakers, and baseball cards.

Nature Smart students learn well when the content may be sorted and classified or is related to natural phenomena.

We show this intelligence as we care for plants and animals. We are also Nature Smart when we are sensitive to environmental issues and the interdependence of living things within ecologies.

People who put their Nature Smarts to work include ecologists, oceanographers, zoologists, astronomers, environmentalists, botanists, veterinarians, and animal trainers.

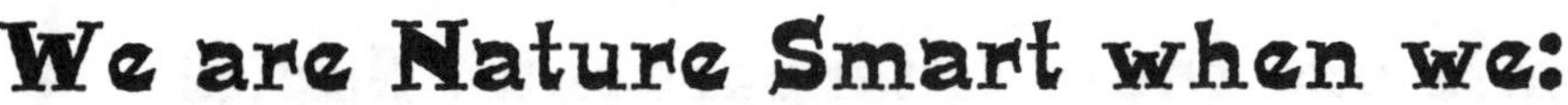

We are Nature Smart when we:

- Care for pets and wild animals
- Notice changes in the environment
- Recognize patterns in nature
- Collect and organize items
- Understand interdependence of living things
- Draw or photograph natural objects
- Trace natural life cycles
- Sort articles from nature
- Protect the environment
- Enjoy being outdoors, camping, hiking, field-trips
- Tame and train animals
- Make fine distinctions between similar types of objects

People Smart

When students use their Interpersonal/Social intelligence, they are being "People Smart."

Students show they are People Smart when they make and maintain friends easily and are sensitive to moods and feelings of others.

Being People Smart includes the ability to understand and work well with others. People Smart also includes the ability to express oneself through cooperative work and leadership skills.

We show this intelligence as we sense moods and temperaments and by accurately interpreting facial expressions, tone of voice, and nonverbal communication. We are People Smart also when we put ourselves in the role of the other and see things from their perspective.

People who put their People Smarts to work include politicians, counselors, actors, mediators, sociologists, nurses, sales people, organizers, and leaders.

We are People Smart when we:

- Understand and respect others
- See the points of view of others
- Display sensitivity to feelings and moods of others
- Focus on other individuals
- Lead and organize others
- Enjoy social gatherings
- Serve as mediators
- Like to work and be with others
- Belong to clubs and organizations
- Listen attentively
- Understand relations among others
- Know why people do what they do

Intrapersonal

Self Smart

When students use their Intrapersonal/ Introspective intelligence, they are being "Self Smart."

Students show they are self smart when they focus inside themselves and become aware of their feelings, memories, goals, dreams, fantasies, strengths, ideas, values, and beliefs.

Being self smart includes constructing an accurate perception of oneself. Self smart also includes the ability to express oneself through planning and setting goals and enjoying private time to think and reflect.

We show this intelligence as we articulate our feelings and act with self-confidence. We are self smart also when we explore our values and beliefs.

People who put their self smarts to work include psychologists, psychiatrists, philosophers, and spiritual, moral, and religious leaders.

We are Self Smart when we:

- Like quiet time alone
- Analyze our range of emotions
- Express our inner-selves
- Hold strong opinions and beliefs
- Dream, fantasize, recall memories
- Maintain self-confidence
- Know our own strengths and weaknesses
- Set goals
- Motivate and direct ourselves
- Think about our own thinking
- Work independently
- Take time to process information

Top 10 Reasons to Care About Multiple Intelligences

You Will:

1. Better prepare students for tomorrow's complex, interdependent world.
2. Make your curriculum accessible to all students.
3. Make your content engaging and exciting for all students.
4. Recognize the intelligences in yourself and your students.
5. Teach students to recognize and value their own unique pattern of intelligences.
6. Foster among students an appreciation, respect, and caring for others.
7. Help students master the content by using their natural strengths.
8. Develop the various facets of each intelligence in each student.
9. Create a more caring, enthusiastic class climate.
10. Rediscover the joy of teaching.

Multiple Intelligences

Structures & Activities Table

* Also involved
** Developed
*** Strongly developed

Structures	Word	Logic/Math	Art/Space	Music	Body	Nature	People	Self
Blind Sequencing	***	***	***		*	**	**	
Draw A Gambit	***						**	
Draw What I Write	***	*	***				**	
Fan-N-Pick	**				*		**	**
Guided Imagery	**		***					*
Jigsaw Problem Solving	**	***			*		**	
Logic Line-Ups	**	***	**		**	*	***	
Lyrical Lessons	*	***		***			*	
Same-Different	***	***	***			***	***	
Sequencing	**	***	**		*	*	**	

Students work in teams to sequence cards.

Multiple Intelligences

- ★★★ Verbal/Linguistic
- ★★★ Logical/Mathematical
- ★★★ Visual/Spatial
- Musical/Rhythmic
- ★ Bodily/Kinesthetic
- ★★ Naturalist
- ★★ Interpersonal
- Intrapersonal

Steps
1. Cards are dealt out, at least one per student.
2. Student One describes one of his or her cards, keeping it hidden.
3. All students discuss where the card belongs in the sequence. Consensus is reached before the card is placed in the sequence, face-down.
4. In turn, each student describes their card and it is placed face-down in the sequence.
5. Students turn over cards, check sequence for correctness and celebrate.

Help!

As Goldilocks was telling her Once Upon a Time story from her clue cards, she dropped them. She vaguely remembers visiting the house of the three bears, sampling chairs, porridge, beds, and falling asleep.

Each teammember will help Goldilocks place her cards back in order. The first student describes one picture card from the story, then places it in order face down. Teammates take turns each placing a card. Each time teammates listen, discuss, and decide whether the card is in the correct order. In the end, the team turns over all the cards to make sure they are in the correct sequence. When they are correct, the team celebrates!

Answers on page 250

Goldilocks

Cut out Cards

Goldilocks

Cut out Cards

Step 1:

Read The Napping House to your students. This classic treasure book is written by Audrey Wood. The story comes to life through each marvelous full-color illustration by Don Wood. It is a simple story of a quiet house where everyone is sleeping. This gentle rhyming tale changes pace when a wakeful flea enters the story.

Step 2:

Give Blind Sequencing directions; run off all 15 cards for each team. Set your students up to become cooperating detectives as they each give oral clues and sequence the clue cards face down. Can they describe and place the cards in the order of the events in the story?

Step 3:

Students play "Blind Sequencing."

Answers on page 251

The Napping
Cut out Cards
Cut out all 15
house cards.
Pass them out
face down to
teammembers.
Play "Blind
Sequencing."

The Napping
Cut out Cards

The Napping
Cut out Cards

The Napping
cut out cards

Together can you remake the Crazy Quilt?

Step 1: Each team receives a set of eight quilts.

Step 2: Shuffle and pass out face down, two per person.

Cut out cards

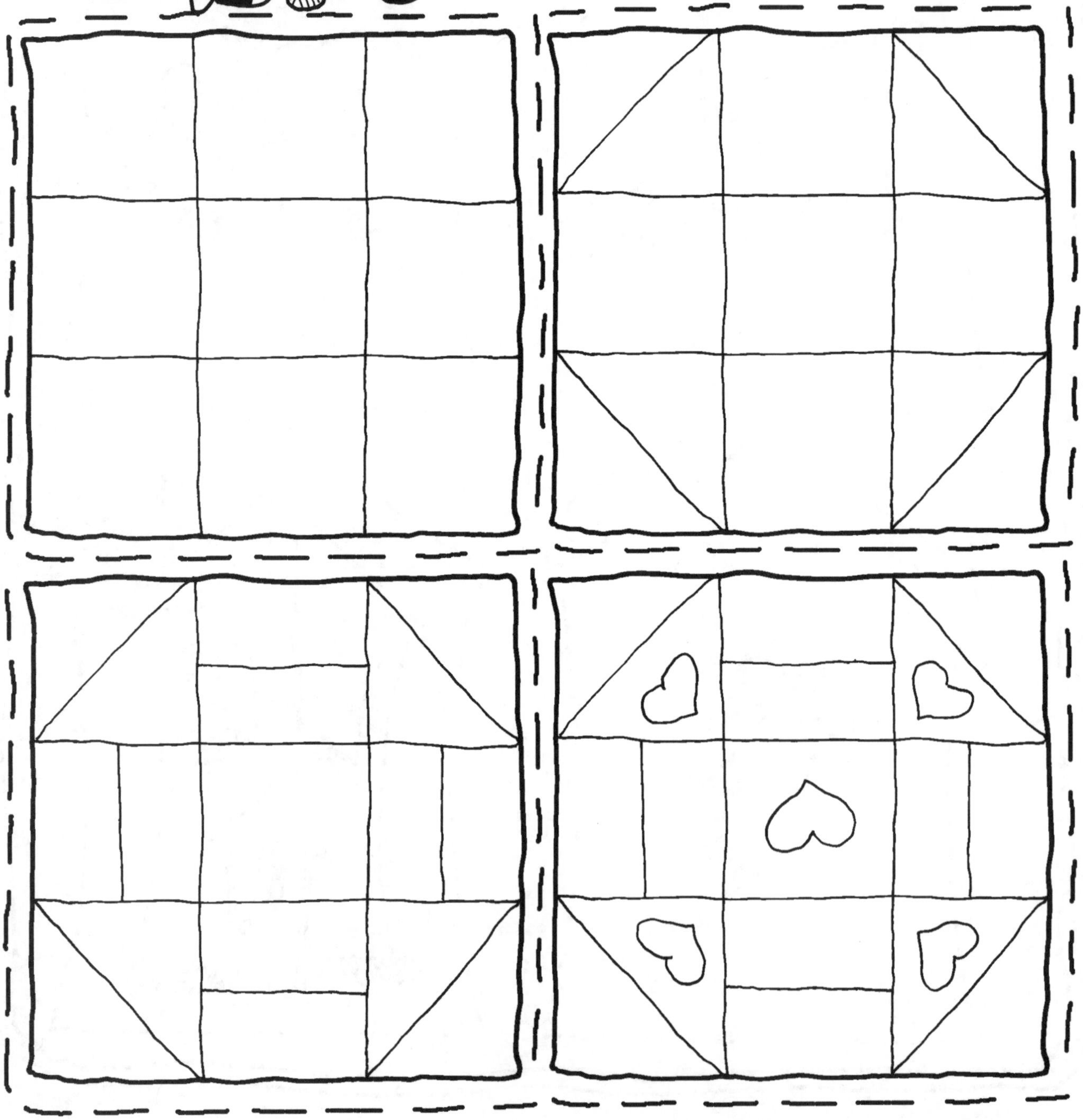

cut out cards

Can you build the schoolhouse as a team?
Cut out cards

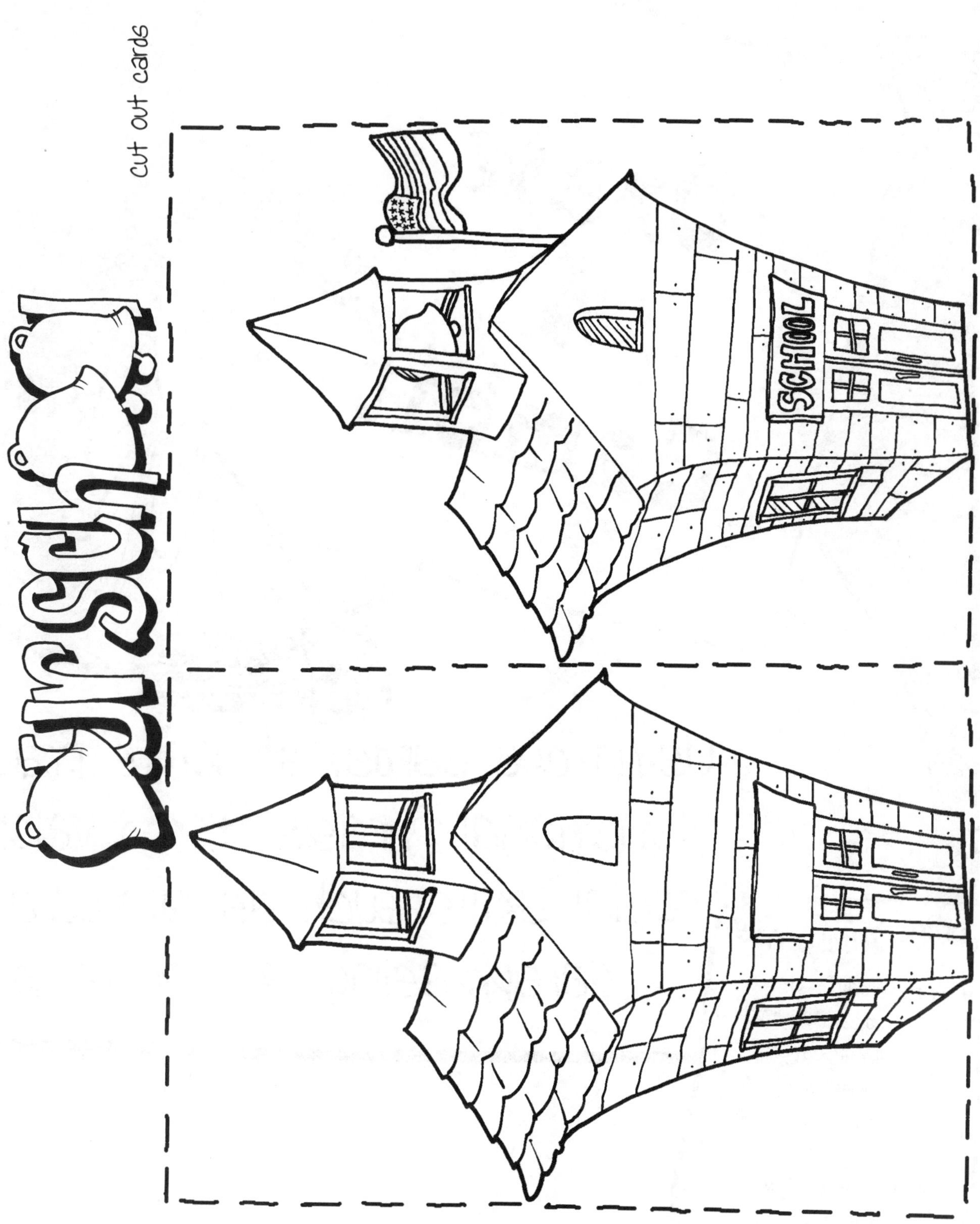
cut out cards
SCHOOL

Using cue cards, students practice functional phrases for developing social skills such as appreciating, paraphrasing, and praising.

Multiple Intelligences

★★★ Verbal/Linguistic
Logical/Mathematical
Visual/Spatial
Musical/Rhythmic
Bodily/Kinesthetic
Naturalist
★★ Interpersonal
Intrapersonal

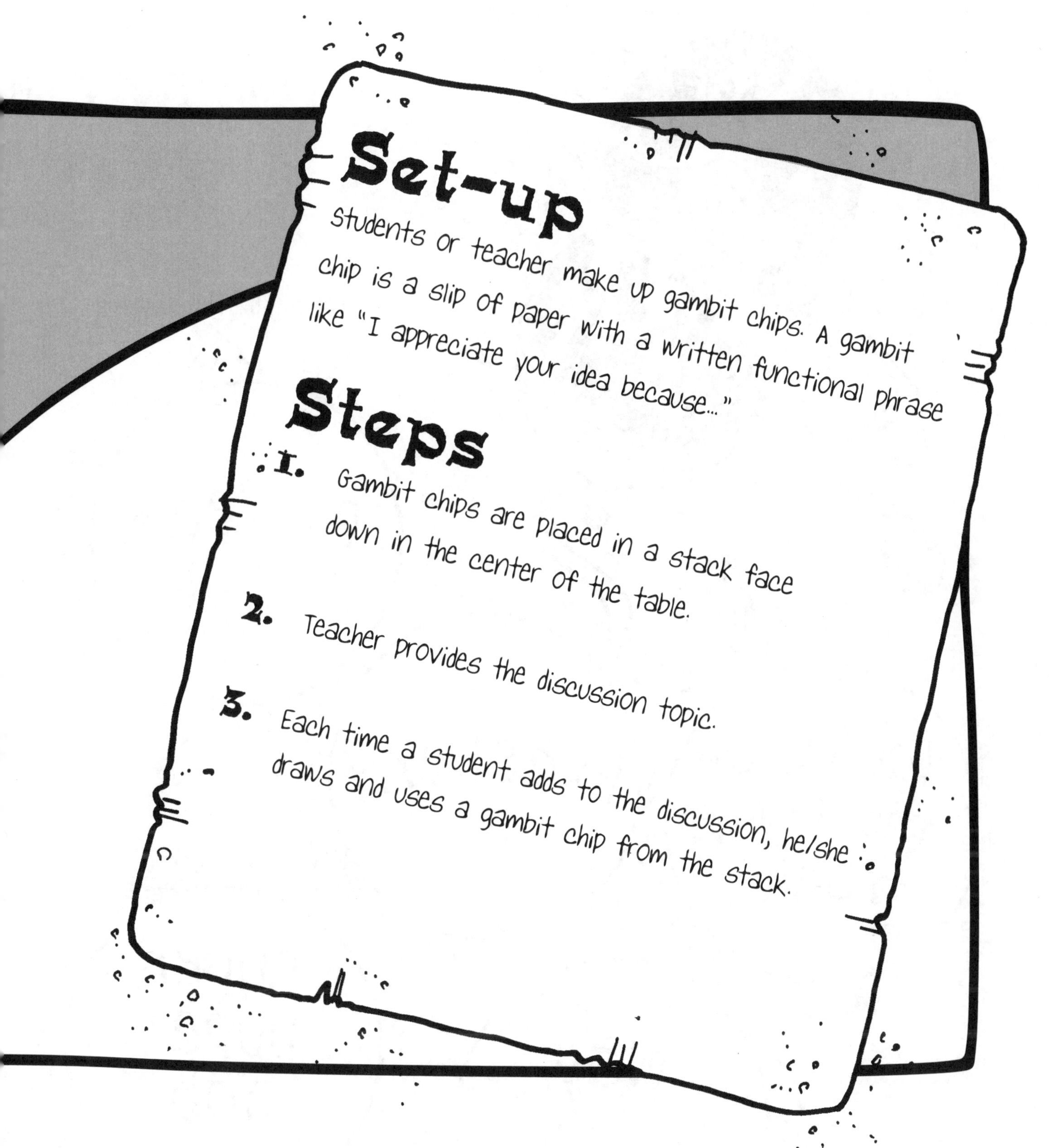
Set-up
Students or teacher make up gambit chips. A gambit chip is a slip of paper with a written functional phrase like "I appreciate your idea because..."
Steps
1. Gambit chips are placed in a stack face down in the center of the table.
2. Teacher provides the discussion topic.
3. Each time a student adds to the discussion, he/she draws and uses a gambit chip from the stack.

Perfect
Praisers
cut out the balloons
perfect
You're on the right track!
Excellent
Super Duper Job
Way to go!

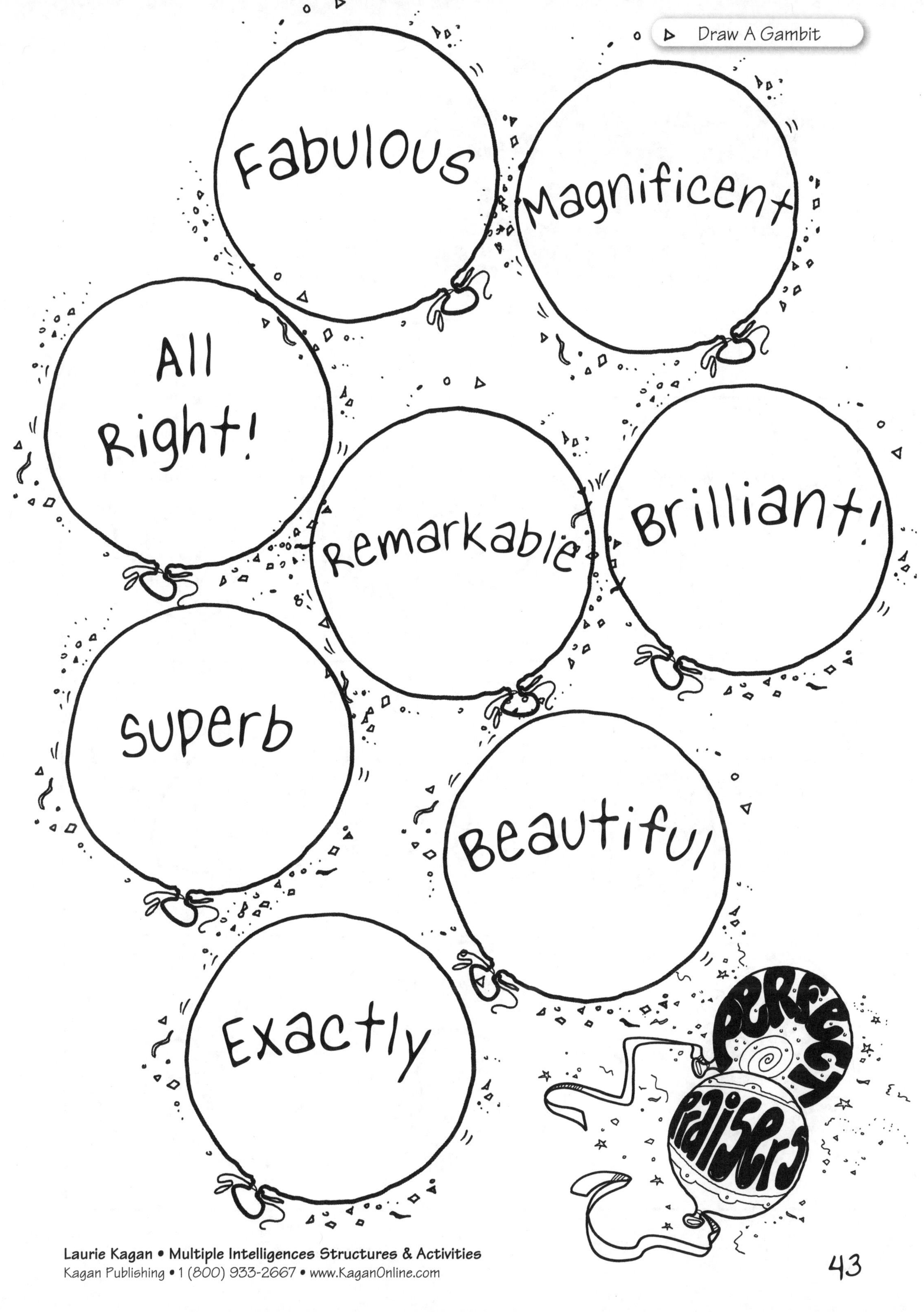
Fabulous
Magnificent
All Right!
Remarkable
Brilliant!
Superb
Beautiful
Exactly
Perfectly Praisers

Paraphrase Gambits
cut out cards
In other words...
So what you're saying is...
All in all...
So you mean that...
If I understand you correctly...
You said...
To sum up...
Let me rephrase that...
In a nutshell...

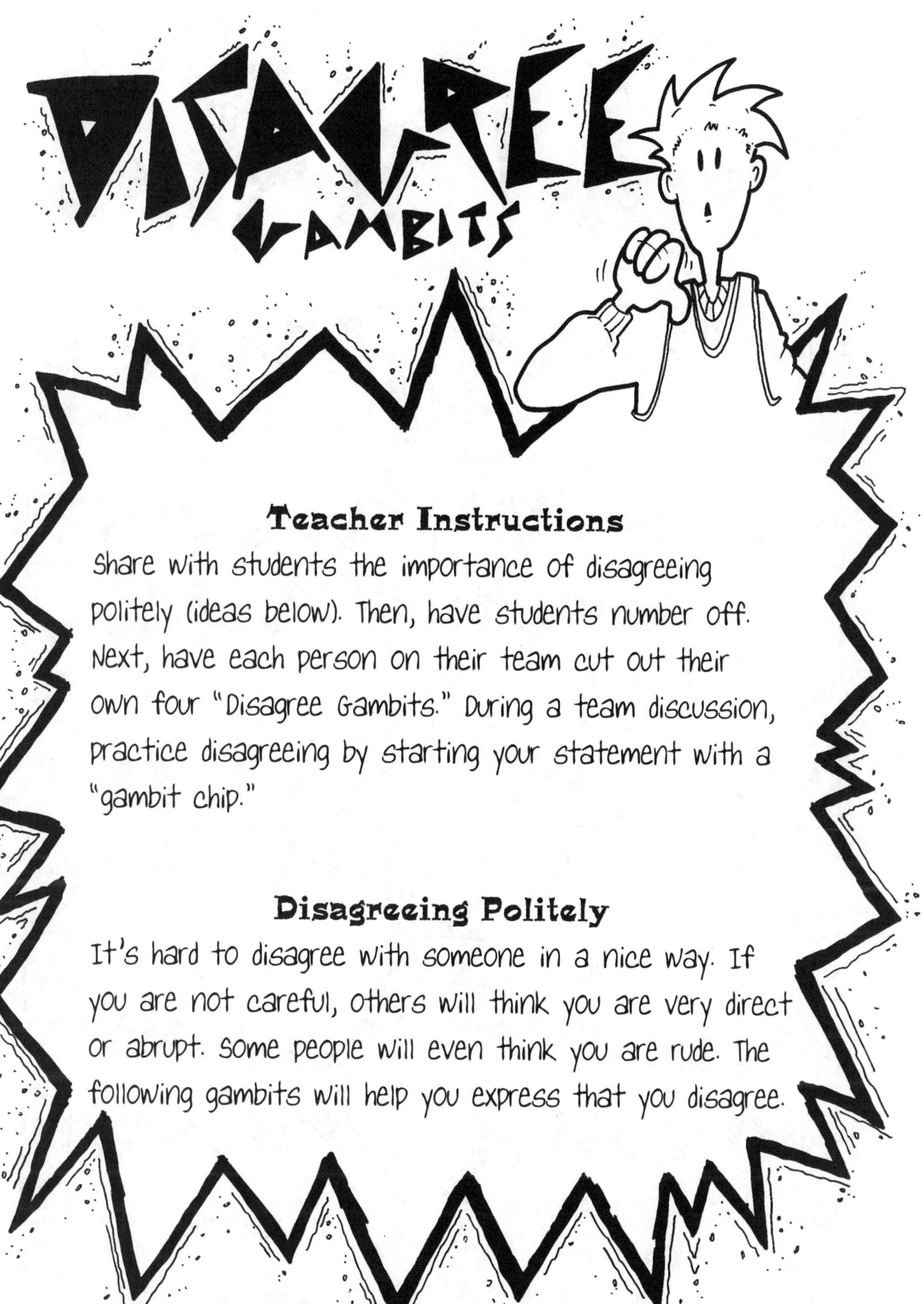

Teacher Instructions

Share with students the importance of disagreeing politely (ideas below). Then, have students number off. Next, have each person on their team cut out their own four "Disagree Gambits." During a team discussion, practice disagreeing by starting your statement with a "gambit chip."

Disagreeing Politely

It's hard to disagree with someone in a nice way. If you are not careful, others will think you are very direct or abrupt. Some people will even think you are rude. The following gambits will help you express that you disagree.

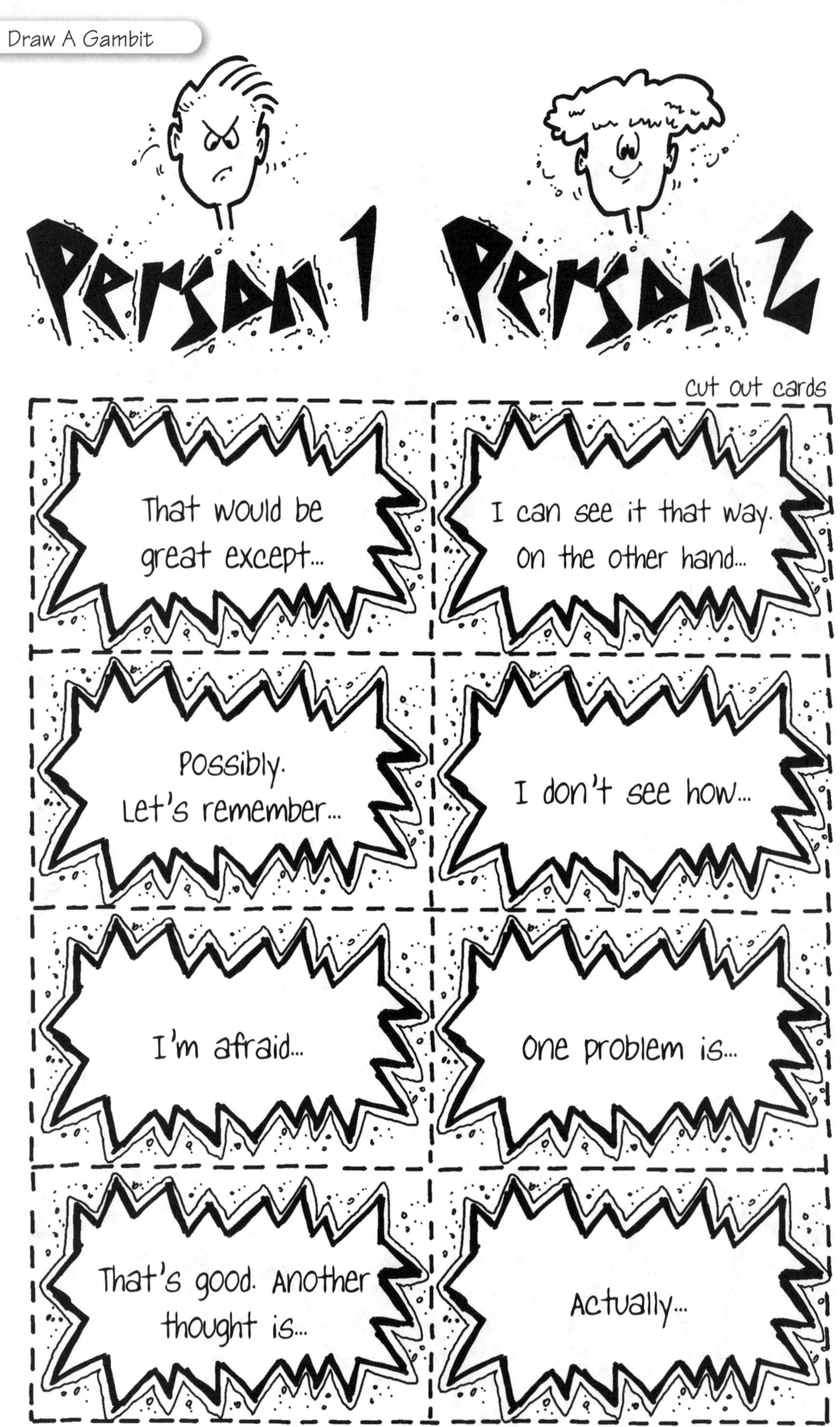
Person 1
Person 2
cut out cards
That would be great except...
I can see it that way. On the other hand...
Possibly. Let's remember...
I don't see how...
I'm afraid...
One problem is...
That's good. Another thought is...
Actually...

Person 3
Person 4
cut out cards
Yes, but don't forget...
It may sound strange, but I think...
What bothers me...
Not everyone will agree with me, but I believe...
I doubt...
That's probably true, but one thing to think about is...
Look at it this way...
I respectfully disagree. I think...

What do U think...
All ideas count!
Use an opinion gambit
before you share your idea.
cut out lightbulbs
What I have in mind is...
I have an idea!...
Mm, that's difficult. Let me see...
I think...
I wonder if...

What Do U think
cut out lightbulbs
I suppose...
In my opinion...
I'm fairly certain that...
How shall I put it...
The best way I can answer that is...
Have you thought about...

COACHING gambits...
If someone doesn't understand...
Use a gambit chip and help them get it right.
cut out cards
Yes, but don't forget...
Okay so far?
Watch the way I...
Do you understand?
How come...?
You're close...
That part's correct, now let's look at...
Please restate how...
What part do you need help with?
Tell me how you...

As ideas are shared, practice "requesting explanations!"

Use the gambit strips

cut out cards

can you explain why...?	can you please help me with...
I don't understand why...	Would you please explain...
Why is it that...?	I'd really like to know...
How come...?	I need help understanding...
Does this mean...?	I'd be appreciative if you could explain...

Students practice written communication skills and get immediate feedback from teammates.

Multiple Intelligences

- ★★★ Verbal/Linguistic
- ★ Logical/Mathematical
- ★★★ Visual/Spatial
- Musical/Rhythmic
- Bodily/Kinesthetic
- Naturalist
- ★★ Interpersonal
- Intrapersonal

Steps
1. Teacher states the rules (e.g. "Draw a noun using six shapes, two must be circles").
2. Teacher models and explains directions.
3. Students draw.
4. Students write directions for a partner to recreate their picture.
5. Students finish, stand, pair up, and sit down side-by-side with their new partner.
6. Partners exchange directions and draw what is written.
7. Partners reveal original drawings and edit to eliminate discrepancies.
8. Partners stand, find new partners, exchange edited directions, and draw from edited version.
9. Partners reveal original drawings, re-edit to eliminate discrepancies.

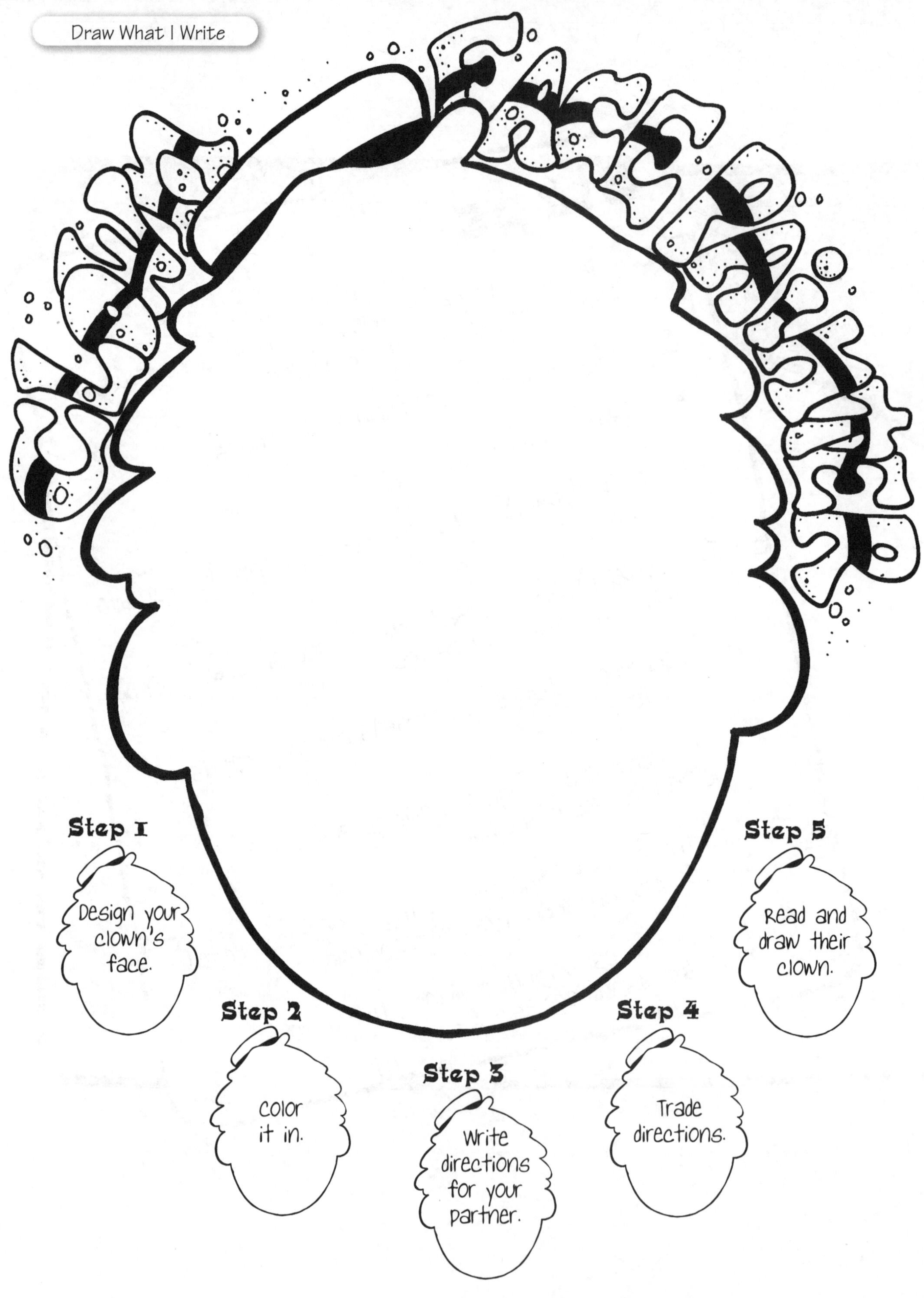
Clown Face Painting
Step 1
Design your clown's face.
Step 2
Color it in.
Step 3
Write directions for your partner.
Step 4
Trade directions.
Step 5
Read and draw their clown.

Clown Face Painter

Write directions clearly

Person I

Look at each step below. Write down clear step-by-step directions. Do not mention it's a <u>bear</u>! When you are finished, find your partner and trade directions only. Read your partner's directions, then on a clean sheet of paper draw the animal described. When done, compare pictures and discuss, "Could the directions have been clearer? How?"

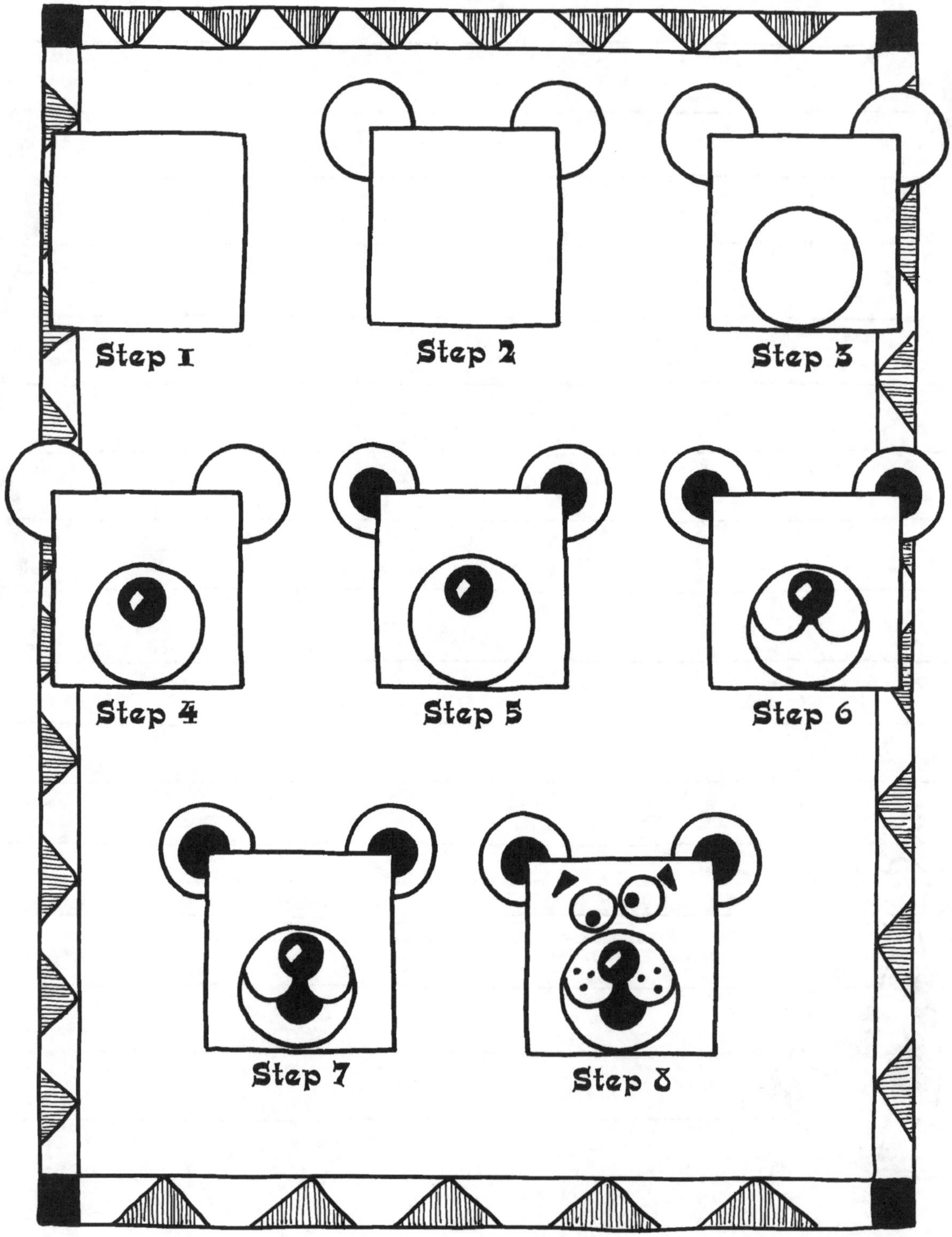

Step 1

Step 2

Step 3

Step 4

Step 5

Step 6

Step 7

Step 8

Giraffe

Person 2

Look at each step below. Write down clear step-by-step directions. Do not mention it's a giraffe! When you are finished, find your partner and trade directions only. Read your partner's directions, then on a clean sheet of paper draw the animal described. When done, compare pictures and discuss, "Could the directions have been clearer? How?"

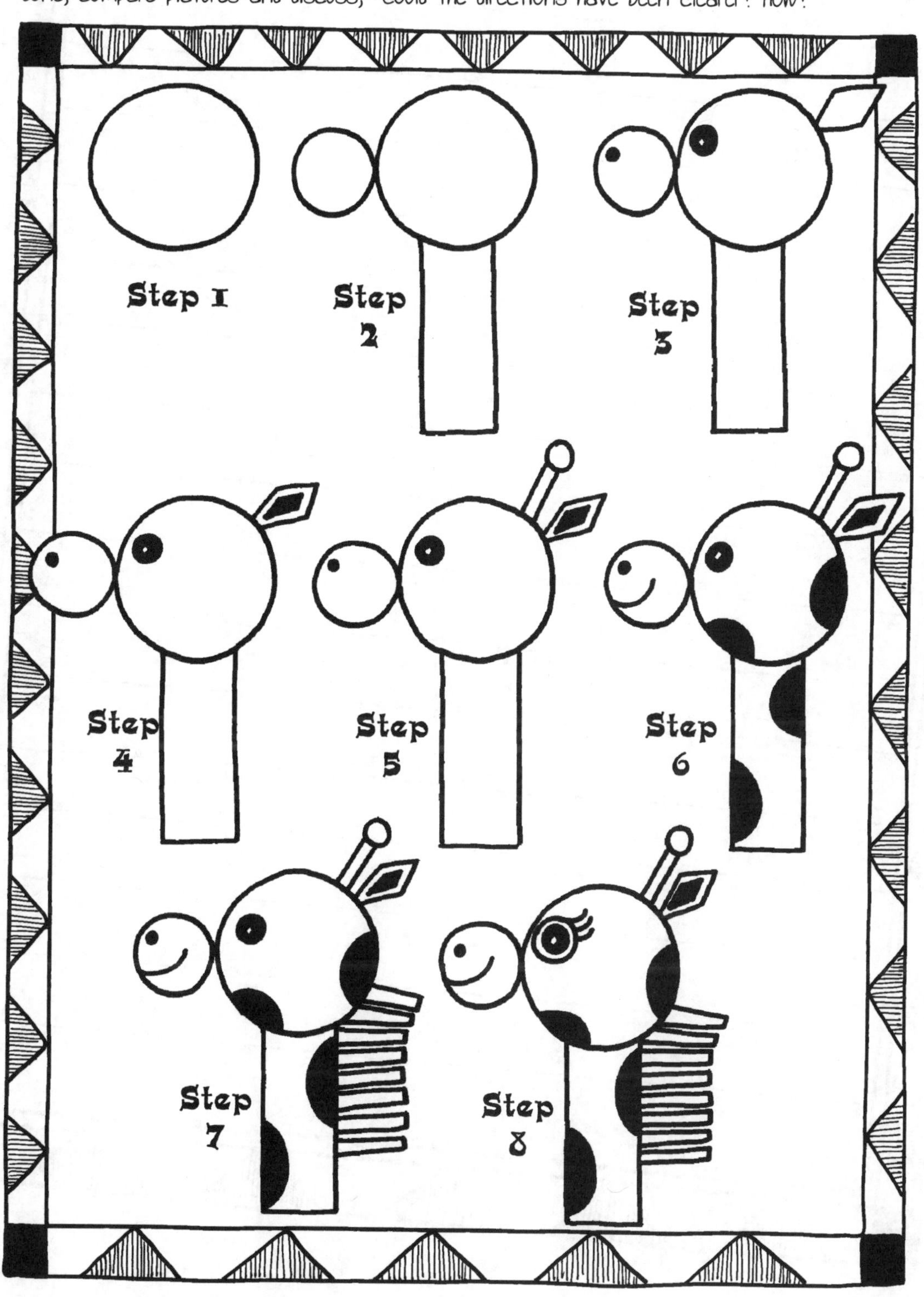

Describe your animal in clear, step-by-step directions.

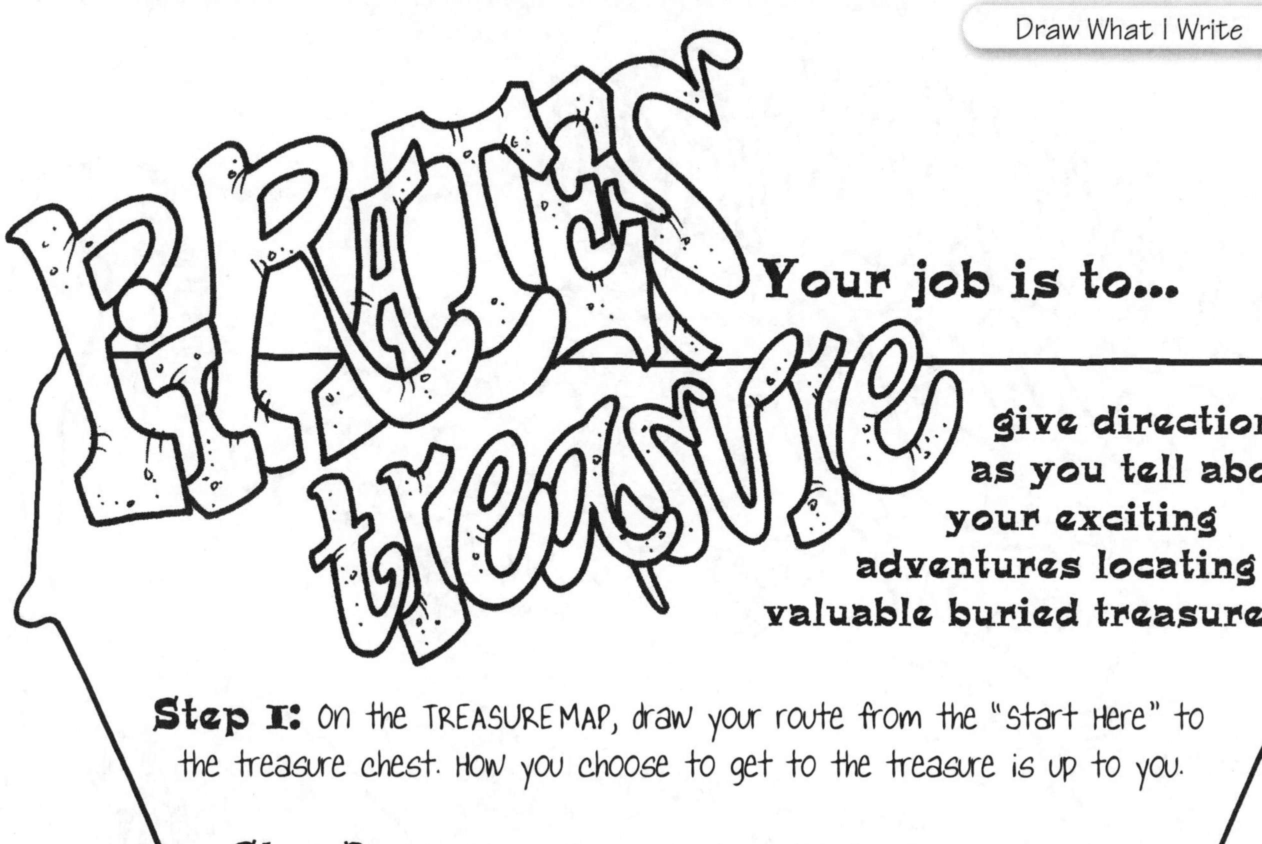

Your job is to...

give directions as you tell about your exciting adventures locating the valuable buried treasure.

Step 1: On the TREASURE MAP, draw your route from the "Start Here" to the treasure chest. How you choose to get to the treasure is up to you.

Step 2: On your SCROLL write down the directions. Remember to use the symbols N, E, S, and W on the compass rose as you explain your detailed directions.

Step 3: Trade your directions with a classmate. As you read your partner's directions, draw on a clean treasure map the trail your partner took that led him or her to the treasure.

- **Advanced:** Draw a scale on your map showing one inch equals 10 miles!

Treasure Map
Start X Here
para reef
island
coin hill
Jolly Roger
sunken ship
restless river
lonesome lake
mistic mountain
prize palms
pirate ship
balanced barrels
rapid river
treasure chest
bottle cove
N
W
E
S

Pirates Treasure

Draw your route to the treasure on the map and write the directions on this scroll!

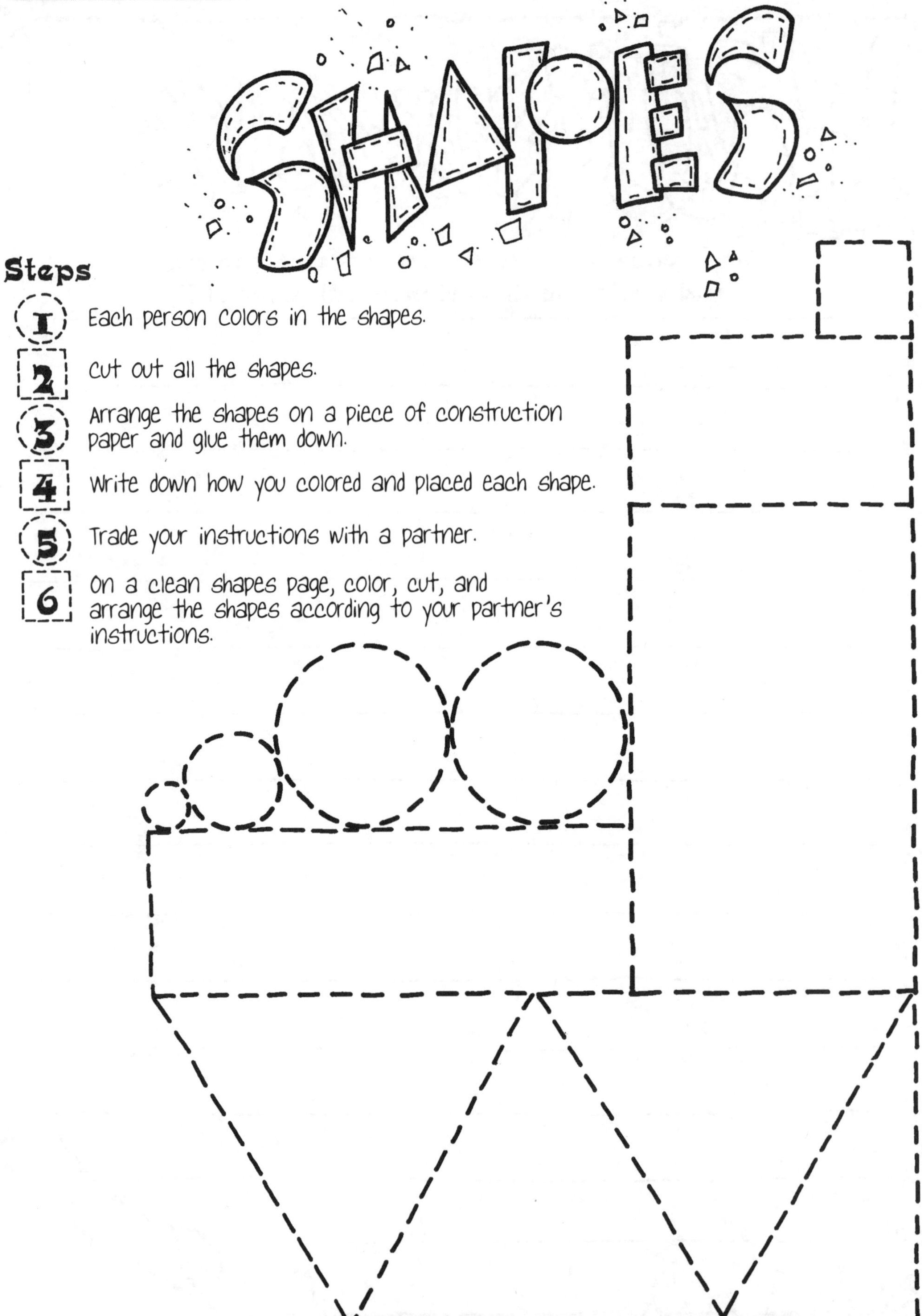

Steps

1. Each person colors in the shapes.
2. Cut out all the shapes.
3. Arrange the shapes on a piece of construction paper and glue them down.
4. Write down how you colored and placed each shape.
5. Trade your instructions with a partner.
6. On a clean shapes page, color, cut, and arrange the shapes according to your partner's instructions.

SHAPES
1.
2.
3.
4.
5.
6.
7.
8.
9.
10.
11.
12.
13.
14.

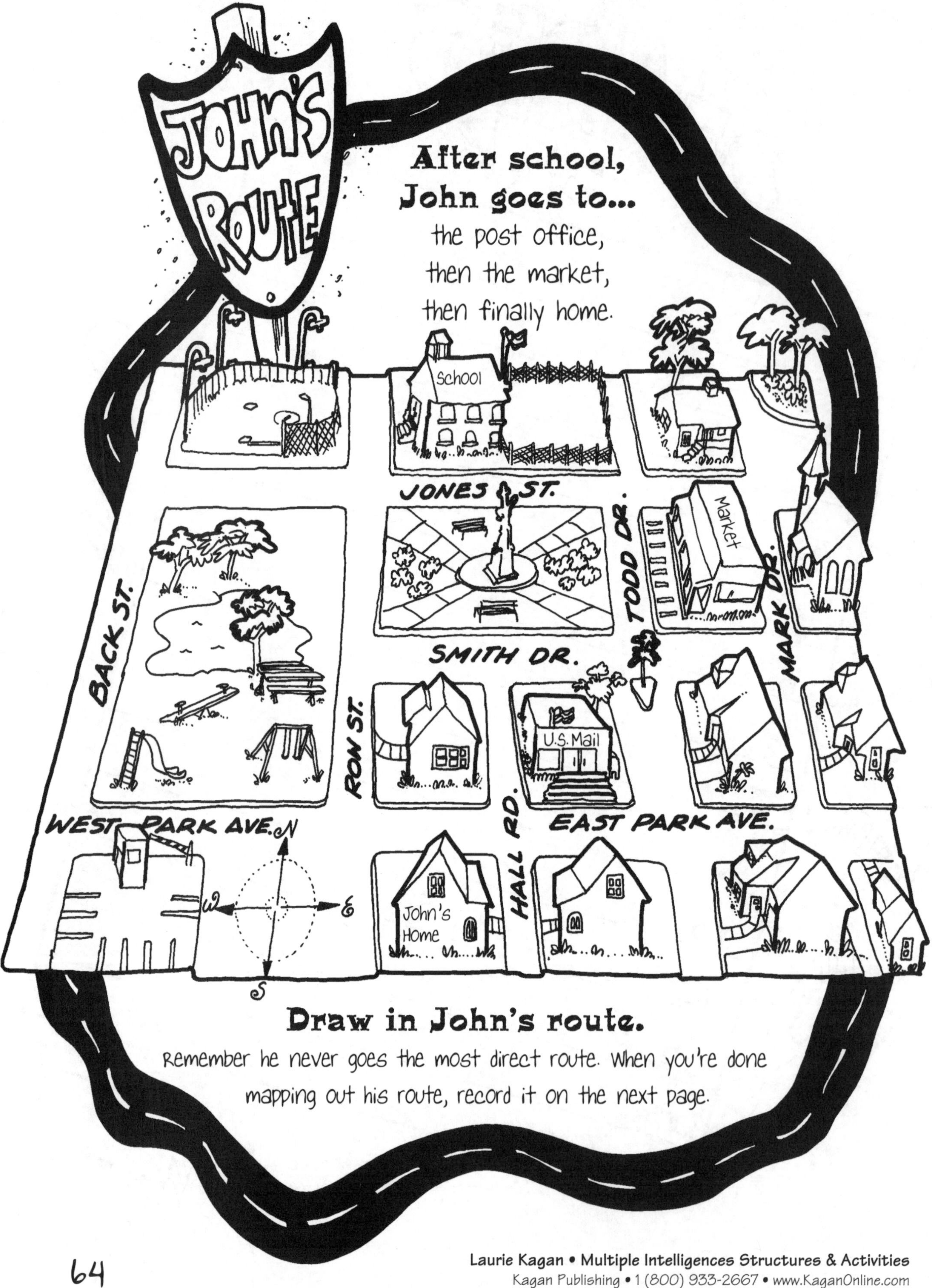

Laurie Kagan • Multiple Intelligences Structures & Activities
Kagan Publishing • 1 (800) 933-2667 • www.KaganOnline.com

JOHN'S ROUTE

Write down John's route.

When done, trade directions and your partner will attempt to draw his or her route from your description. Good Luck!

Name

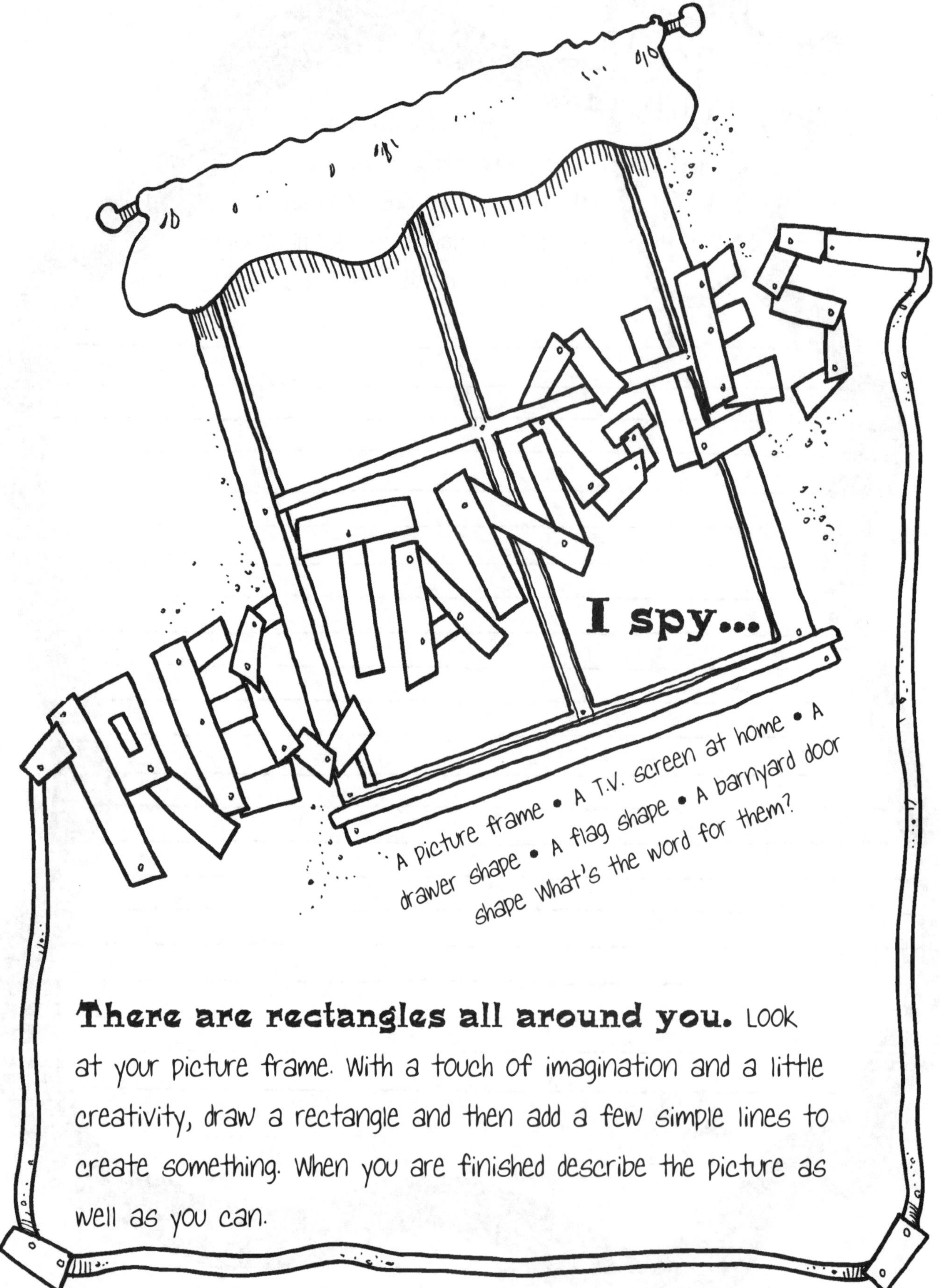

There are rectangles all around you. Look at your picture frame. With a touch of imagination and a little creativity, draw a rectangle and then add a few simple lines to create something. When you are finished describe the picture as well as you can.

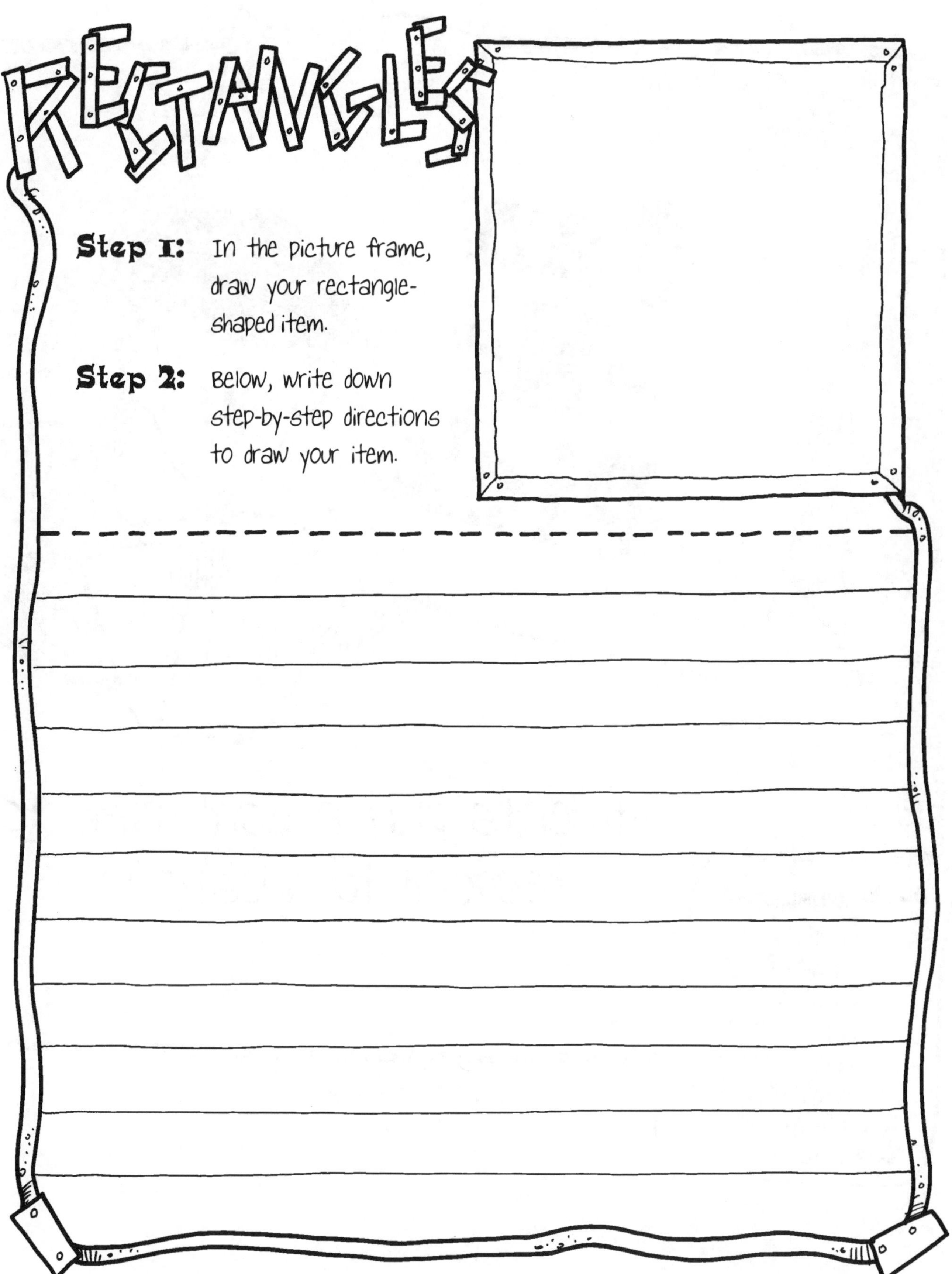
RECTANGLES
Step 1: In the picture frame, draw your rectangle-shaped item.
Step 2: Below, write down step-by-step directions to draw your item.

Students play a card game to respond to questions.

Multiple Intelligences

★★ Verbal/Linguistic
Logical/Mathematical
Visual/Spatial
Musical/Rhythmic
★ Bodily/Kinesthetic
Naturalist
★★ Interpersonal
★★ Intrapersonal

Set up
One set of questions per team.
Steps
1. Student One holds question cards in a fan and says, "Pick a card, any card!"
2. Student Two picks a card, reads it out loud, allows five seconds of think time.
3. Student Three answers the question.
4. Student Four checks, praises, helps, or paraphrases.
5. Students rotate roles one clockwise for each new round.

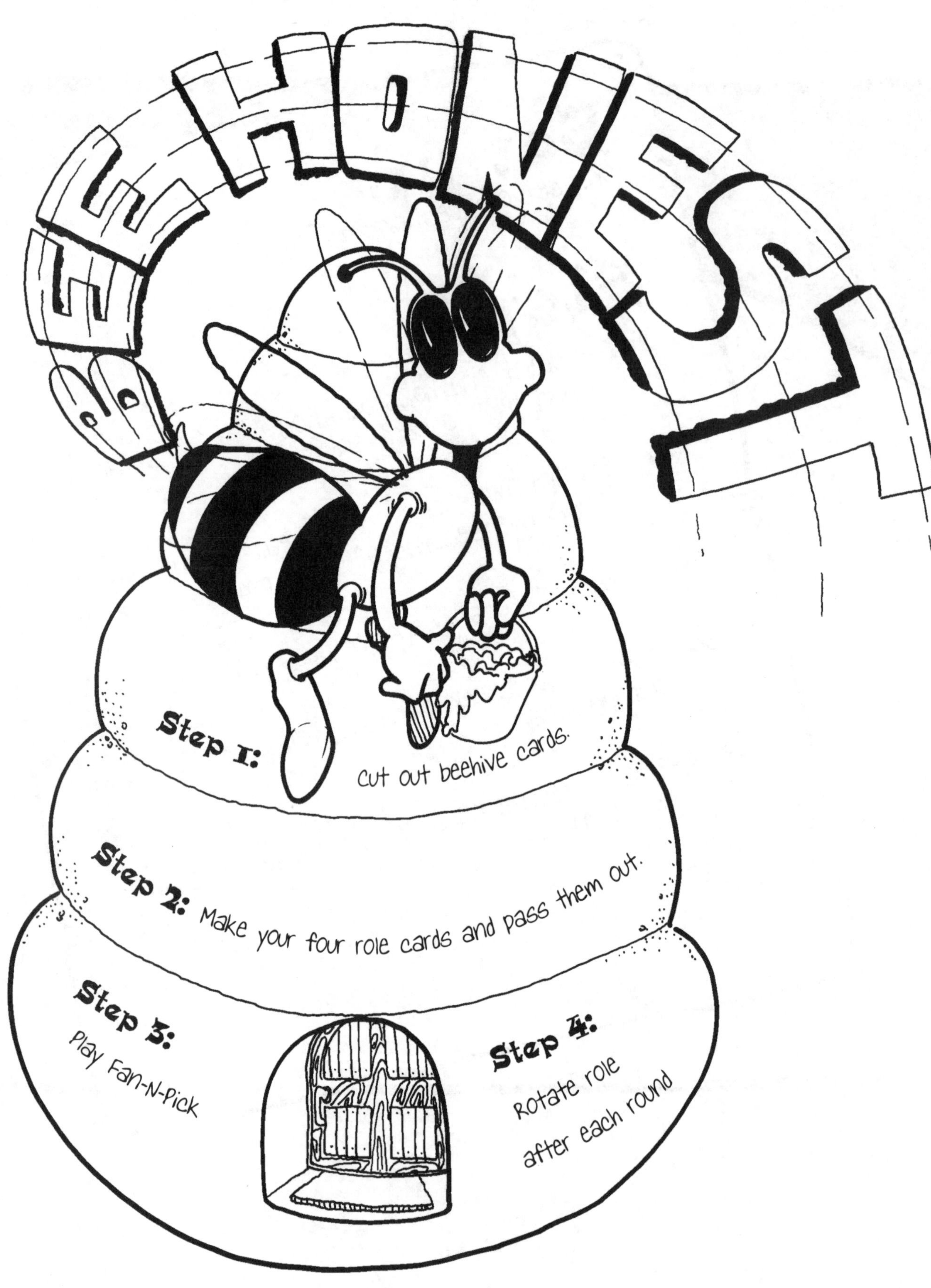
BEE HONEST
Step 1:
Cut out beehive cards.
Step 2: Make your four role cards and pass them out.
Step 3:
Play Fan-N-Pick
Step 4:
Rotate role
after each round

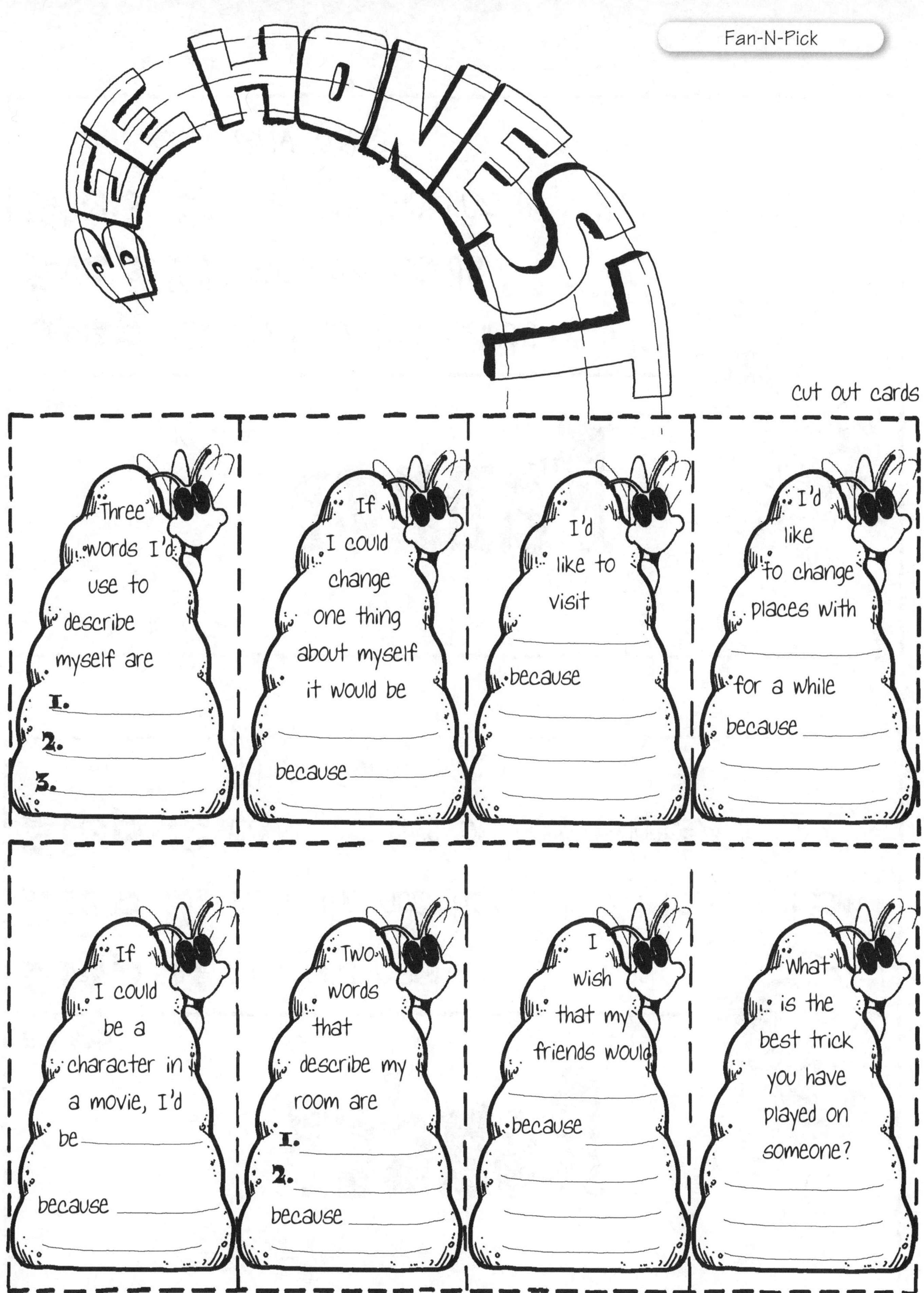
BE HONEST
cut out cards
Three words I'd use to describe myself are
1.
2.
3.
If I could change one thing about myself it would be
because
I'd like to visit
because
I'd like to change places with
for a while because
If I could be a character in a movie, I'd be
because
Two words that describe my room are
1.
2.
because
I wish that my friends would
because
What is the best trick you have played on someone?

Step 1: Shuffle the cards.

Step 2: Fan the cards.

Step 3: Say to the reader, "Pick a card, any card!"

First

Fanner

Step 1: Pick one card.

Step 2: Read the question out loud to your team.

Step 3: Count to five on your fingers for "Think Time."

Second

Reader

Step 1: Think about your answer.
Remember to "bee honest."

Step 2: Tell your teammates your answer.

Third

Answerer

Step 1: Show appreciation to

the answerer.

Fourth

Praiser

giving
TREE
Read The Giving Tree by Shel Silverstein, a moving parable about the gift of love.
Why was the apple tree in the story called The Giving Tree?
1
In what ways did the tree give?
2
Why do yo think the tree loved the boy? How did the tree show love for the boy?
3
Why do you think the boy loved the tree? How did the boy show his love for the tree?
4
cut out logs
How could the boy have shown he was thankful?
5

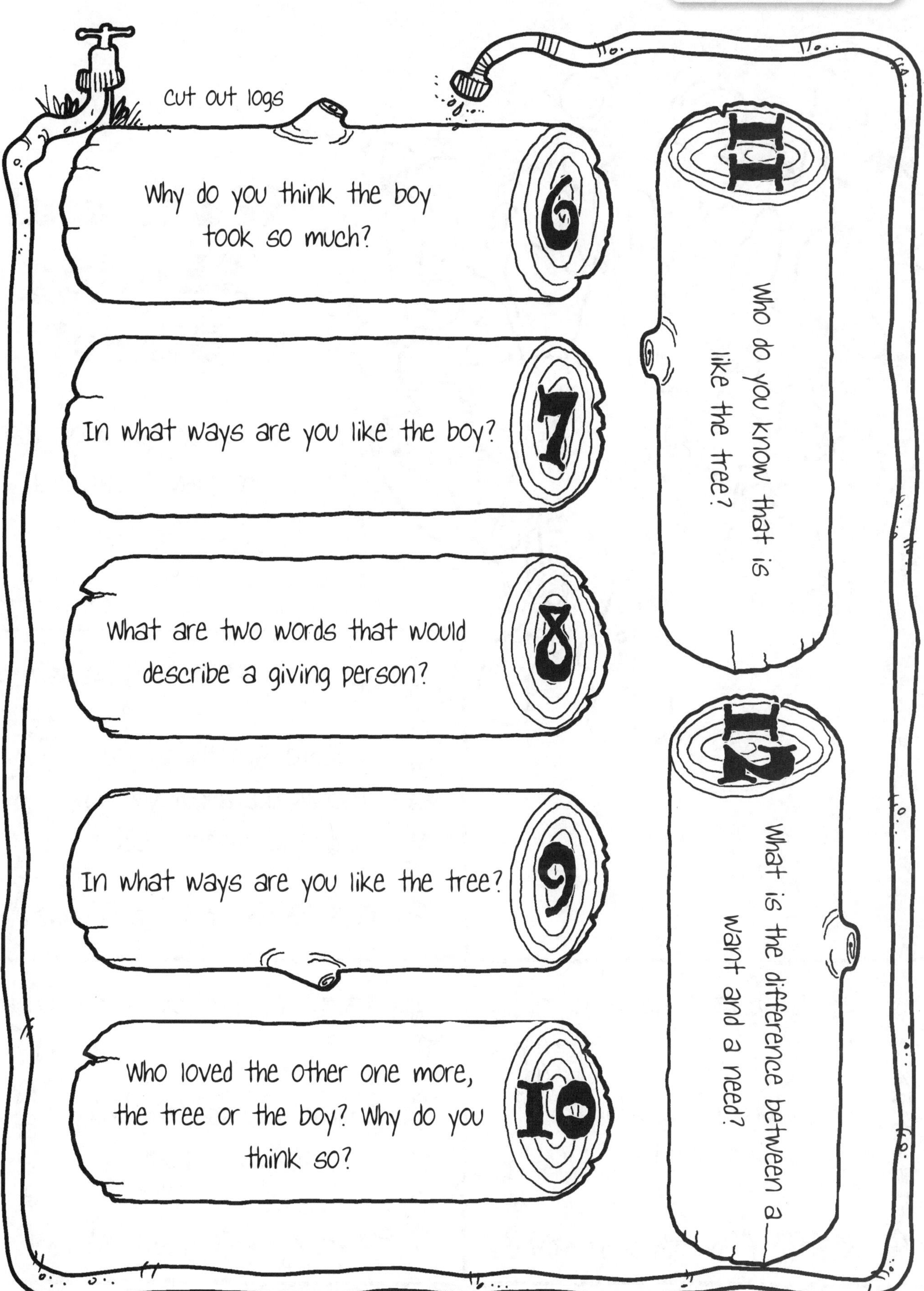
cut out logs
Why do you think the boy took so much?
6
In what ways are you like the boy?
7
What are two words that would describe a giving person?
8
In what ways are you like the tree?
9
Who loved the other one more, the tree or the boy? Why do you think so?
10
Who do you know that is like the tree?
11
What is the difference between a want and a need?
12

Shining Stars
We are all Shining Stars!
Use these question cards to play Fan-N-Pick.
cut out cards
Name two things your friends like about you. Why did you choose those?
Tell about a special birthday you had.
Explain a pleasant memory from your past.

Shining Stars
One of my favorite spots to spend some time is... Explain.
cut out cards
I'm eagerly looking forward to...
Three things I think I'm really good at are...
One of my favorite times of the year is... Because...
What is something special and different about you?

Book Report
Make book reports fun!
Cut out all 12 books on the following pages. When playing Fan-N-Pick, you can pick out your favorite questions, or use all 12. Save the book report Fan-N-Pick cards to use again for another book report.
Person #1: Fan the books like a deck of cards.
Person #2: Pretend you are a "reporter." Ask Person #3 the question.
Person #3: Answer the question.
Person #4: Praise the answerer!
Now rotate roles!

Book Report
cut out books
1
What was your favorite part? Why?
2
Summarize the book/story in one or two sentences.
3
Would you recommend the book/story to another person? Why or Why not?
4
Which character can you identify most closely with? Why?

Book Report
cut out books
5
If you could change any part of the story, what would you change? Why?
6
Come up with a new title. Explain why you named it that.
7
You are going to change places with one character in the book/story. Who would you be? Why that character?
8
Select two characters in the book/story. What are two ways they are alike and two ways they are different?

Book Report
cut out books
9
What are some of the turning points in the book/story?
10
Which character in the story did you like the least? Explain why.
11
Which character in the story did you like most? Explain why.
12
Which one color represents the story? Explain your answer.

The ? Box
Cut out all 18 question boxes. Play Fan-N-Pick!
Box 1
What is your least favorite food?
Why?
Box 2
What would it be like if you had an extra set of arms?
Explain.
Box 3
Which animal is the most beautiful?
Explain.
Box 4
What is the best memory of a vacation you have taken?
Describe.
Box 5
Where is the best hiding place in your house?
Explain.
Box 6
If you could add 4 hours to the 24 hour clock, where would you add it?
Why?

Cut out cards
Box 7
What do you like to do in your free time?
Describe
Box 8
If you could only watch TV one hour a week, what would you watch?
Why?
Box 9
If you had a magic carpet, where would you want it to take you?
Why?
Box 10
Would you rather be a cat or a dog?
Explain.
Box 11
Would you like to have an identical twin?
Why or Why not?
Box 12
What is your favorite dessert?
Describe it.
Box 13
If you had the gift of magic for a day, how would you use it?
Explain.
Box 14
You have become a famous sports star! What do you do?
Explain.
Box 15
Where do you want me to buy you a $100 gift certificate from?
Explain.
Box 16
Tell me about
Box 17
Explain why
Box 18
What is

What famous person would you be? Why?

What name would you like to have if you couldn't have yours? Why?

What is your most important possession? Explain why.

Name one quality you could improve to be a better friend. Why do you think so?

What is your favorite song? Why is it your favorite?

What do you like and dislike about yourself? Name three things you like and three things you dislike.

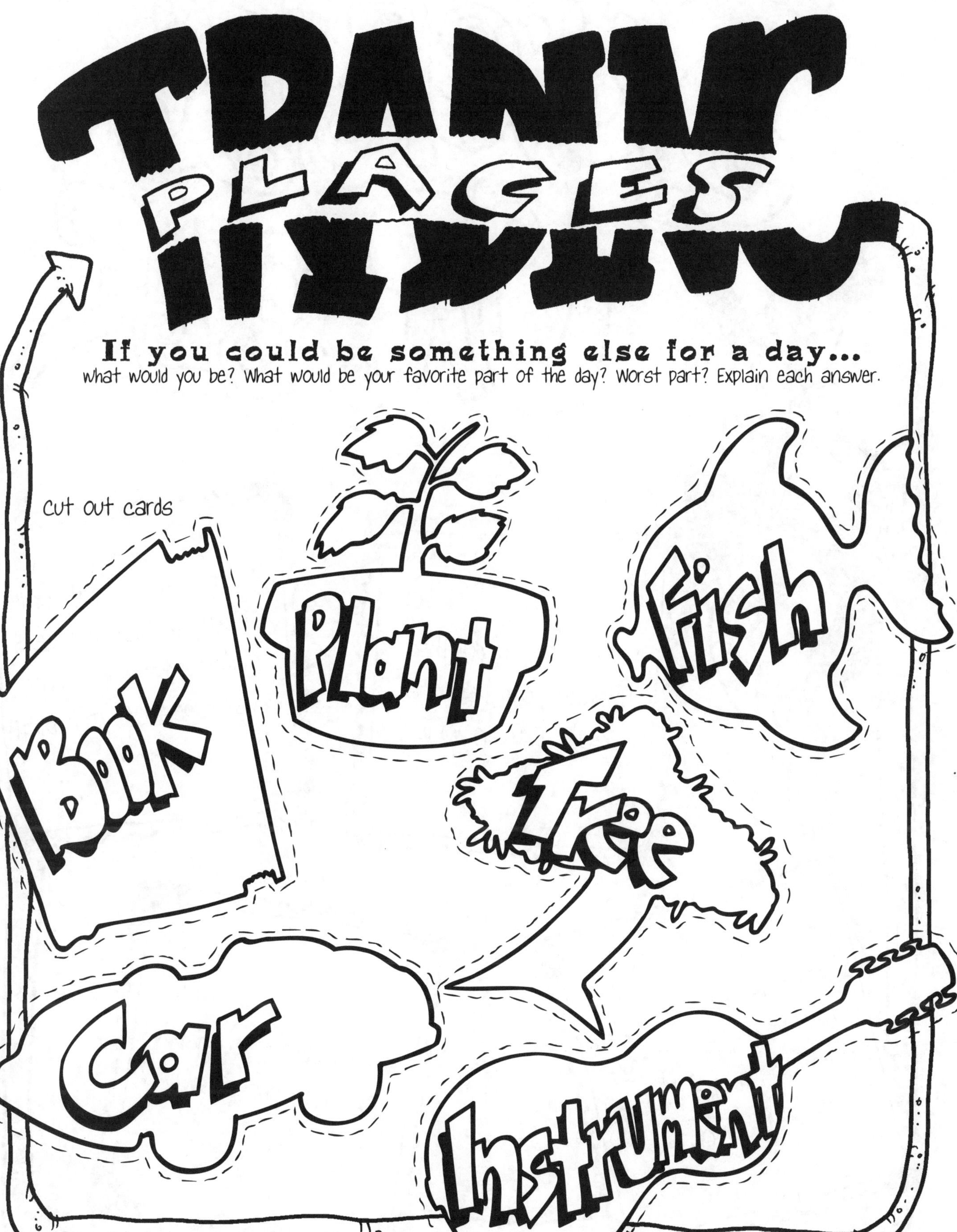
PLACES
If you could be something else for a day...
what would you be? What would be your favorite part of the day? Worst part? Explain each answer.
cut out cards
Book
Plant
Fish
Tree
Car
Instrument

Describe U'rself
cut out cards
What do you do that makes your parents mad? Explain why.
What is your birth order (oldest, middle, youngest, only)? What are three advantages of your birth order?
What is your favorite toy, game, or stuffed animal? Explain why it is your favorite.
What makes you happy? Explain your answer.

cut out cards
What is the bravest thing you have ever done? Explain.
How are you alike or different from your brothers and sisters? Explain.
Finish this statement: I make a good friend because
Are you a good loser? Why or why not?
What are you afraid of? Explain why.
What makes you sad? Explain why.

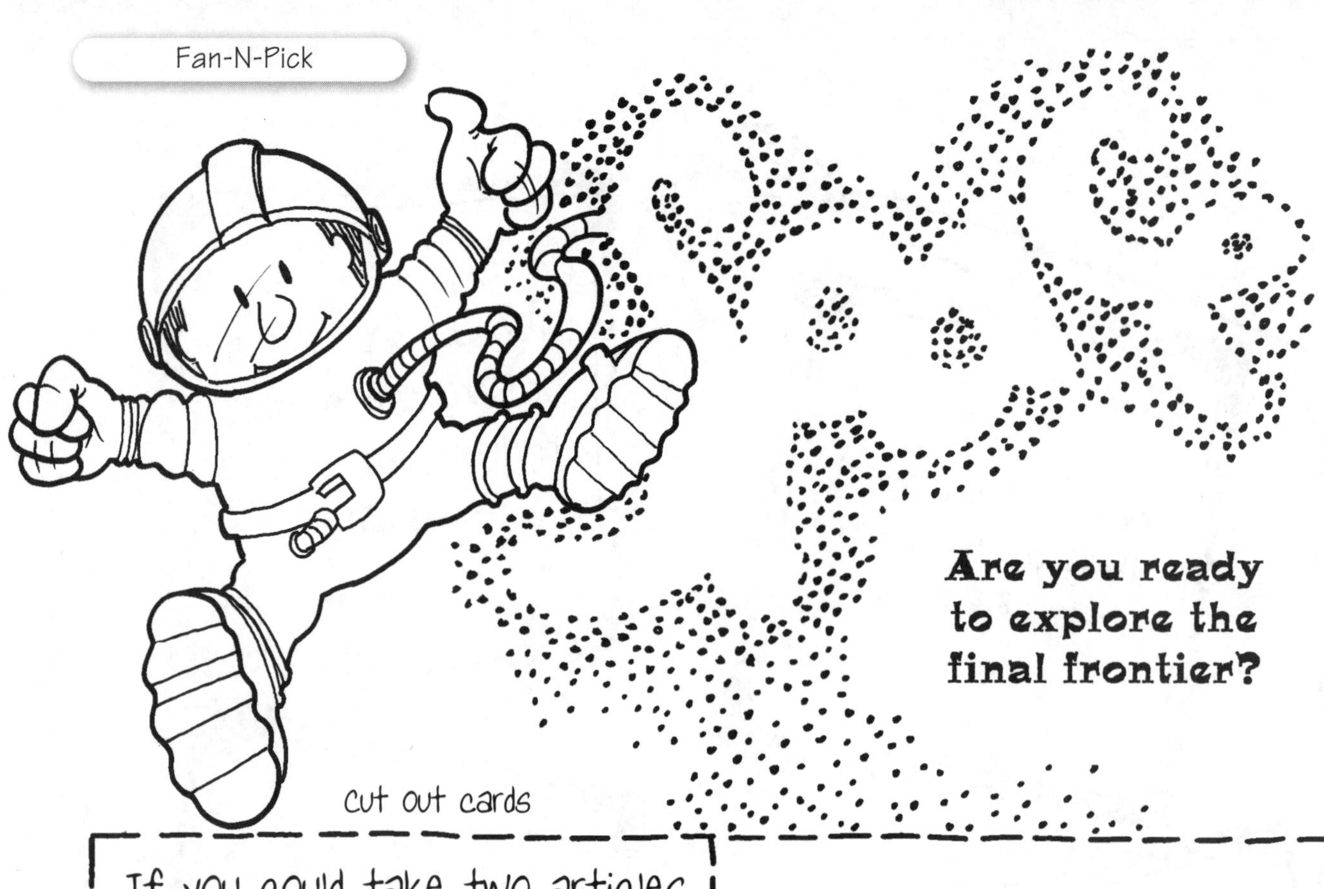

Are you ready to explore the final frontier?

cut out cards

If you could take two articles from your house with you when you move to a space station, what would they be? Why did you select them?	Name eight space words.
If you couldn't live on Earth, on which planet would you most like to live? Justify your answer.	Would you like to travel in space? Why or why not?

cut out cards

Do you think someone you know will travel in space in your lifetime?

Why or why not?

There are risks and benefits of being an astronaut. List three risks and three benefits.

Which is greater?

List five benefits of living on the Earth compared to living on the moon.

What recommendations could you make to improve life on earth?

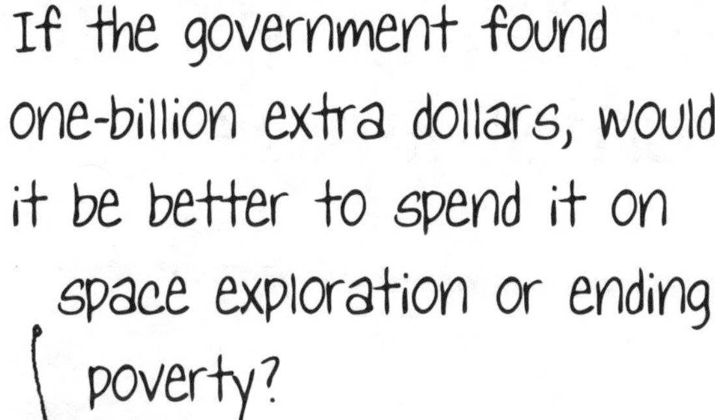

If the government found one-billion extra dollars, would it be better to spend it on space exploration or ending poverty?

Explain your answer.

Name the planets in order from the sun. What method do you use to remember them?

Teacher leads students on an imaginary voyage through their own mental imagery.

Multiple Intelligences

- ★★ Verbal/Linguistic
- Logical/Mathematical
- ★★★ Visual/Spatial
- Musical/Rhythmic
- Bodily/Kinesthetic
- Naturalist
- Interpersonal
- ★ Intrapersonal

Steps
1. Teacher tells students to shut their eyes and get relaxed.
2. Students shut their eyes, get relaxed but alert.
3. As Teacher describes images, students listen and visualize as fully as possible.

Guided Imagery Notes

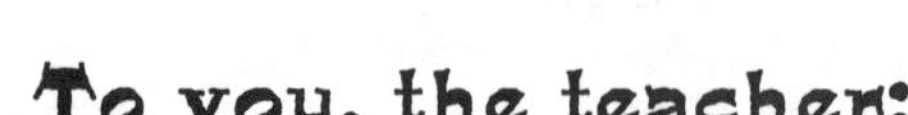

Guided Imagery is like a visualization except that you guide the visualization. You talk, while the students visualize, directing their attention to various things. The same words you would say before a visualization are now said during guided imagery. You may also guide the students to focus on certain things by saying things like, "Now look closer at..." or, "Turn your attention to..." You can even ask the students to engage in a conversation during the guided imagery. Say something like, "Now ask the butterfly where it is going. Listen to what it tells you."

A guided imagery may take the students through a process (steps of a math problem, steps to follow in a science experiment, steps of a swimming flip turn) or on an exploration of a place (what they see in Lincoln's log cabin, what they see in the pond).

It is easiest if you have a prepared script or if you are very familiar with the content. Remember, you are guiding the students to focus on things you hope they will remember.

Riding the Underground railroad
Class...I want you all to close your eyes. Get comfortable. Take a deep breath. Let it out slowly. Now do that again...
The reason I want to get you relaxed is so that nothing will interfere as we go back in time to take a trip on the underground railroad...

Shut your eyes and relax. Get ready for our journey. You will see every detail in your mind's eye. We are going back in time. We are traveling to a different place. You are going to be a different person...

You are a slave on a tobacco plantation during the time of the underground railroad. You are in the tobacco fields, cultivating the plants. It is a hot and humid day, and you have been working hard. You would like to rest but not too far from you is the master's assistant on his horse, his dogs close by. You know to rest would buy you a lash from the whip. You keep working.

In the last few days you have heard talk. You have heard about a brave black woman, Harriet Tubman. The slaves call her "The Conductor." Some have said she is in the area. You know about her. She is the ex-slave who is making daring trips, fearlessly escaping hunters and dogs, leading slaves through swamps and woods, north to freedom. You have heard how some whites have coordinated to help Harriet and her passengers. At great risk to themselves they have formed underground railroad "stations," hidden tunnels and caves under their homes or in the back of their barns to hide Harriet and her passengers on their trip north to freedom. You know that some of those who have sheltered slaves on the passage north have been discovered and hung. You picture being dragged from a basement by those who hunt slaves. You picture cold and hungry slaves being returned to their masters to be whipped in front of everyone on the plantation.

It is evening now, and you are sitting on a log, by a fire. You look at the stars. Without thinking about anything your eyes wander to the North Star. You know Harriet Tubman uses the North Star to guide her and her passengers on the underground railroad. You hum to yourself a song which every slave knows - "Follow the Drinking Gourd." The song contains secret clues which would help guide you on a trip north. You wonder what it would be like to be free.

To your mind comes the picture of the master's assistant today, riding on his horse, using his whip on some of the slaves. Today you escaped the whip, but there have been days you have felt its bitter bite. You remember last month how the master gathered all the slaves to watch John be whipped. John had not bowed as the Master approached. To teach him proper respect and to teach all the other slaves a lesson, John was whipped until he bled. Without thinking, you reach back and feel the scars on your own back. Scars you know will never heal. Scars left by the whip when you were younger and not quick to obey.

As you sit on the log, you are surprised to see John approach. You know he is not supposed to leave his cabin tonight, but John seems almost fearless as he takes a place beside you on the log by the fire. There is an energy in John's body. You wonder how he can be so excited after a long day in the fields and the punishment he has received. John tells you The conductor is coming tomorrow night to the plantation. She is going to take some slaves as passengers on her next trip north. John himself will make the trip. He asks you to join him.

You tell him you must think about it. You look up at the stars, looking north. Then you look out into the woods. You shudder from the cold. You picture being hunted by men on horseback with dogs. You picture wading through the swamps, peeling leeches from your body. You see yourself in the woods, chased by barking dogs. You see yourself cold and hungry, sneaking up on a safe station only to find you cannot stay there because it is being watched.

And then almost like a vision, you see in the flames of the fire a picture of the face of Harriet Tubman herself, The conductor. You picture her with her pistol saying a trip on the underground railroad is a one-way ticket. No one can turn back. To turn back is to risk the lives of the whole group. She holds her pistol and says, no matter how cold, how hungry, how afraid, how lonely for your loved ones, you continue or you die. You shudder as you look into the fire. The night is growing colder.

With John carefully watching your face, you stand, trying to feel the warmth of the fire. You tell John, a trip on the railroad is a trip away from the whip. Toward freedom. But is is a trip away from everything you know. Your whole life you have never traveled more than a few miles from the plantation. You say that to take a trip on the underground railroad means leaving loved ones. Never seeing them again. You shudder again. The night has grown even colder.

You get up and put another log on the fire. Then, slowly, with a tear in your eye, you turn to John and say, "John, I have made up my mind..."

Now class, before you open your eyes, picture what you are going to tell John. See yourself and listen to your own words as you tell him what you have decided. When you are ready, open your eyes, turn to a partner, and tell them what you told John. Will you take the trip on the underground railroad? Tell your partner all the reasons you want to go, and all the fears you have. Tell your partner not just what your decision is, but why.

by Spencer Kagan

Class, I want you all to close your eyes. Get comfortable. Take a deep breath and let it out slowly. Now do that again. The reason I want you to get you relaxed is so that nothing will interfere as we watch a miracle of nature. We are going to watch a large red-brown and black Monarch butterfly turn into a chrysalis...

It is the summer and a female Monarch has found milkweed leaves and has glued its tiny eggs to the leaf. We take out a magnifying glass and look carefully at the eggs. We are surprised to find they are so pretty. They are greenish and shaped like a cone. They have on them neat ribs.

As we are watching, an egg hatches into a tiny green caterpillar. Look at the caterpillar carefully. Look at its green color. Now watch it, it begins doing the main thing caterpillars do: it begins eating. It just keeps eating and eating. Watch as it takes a bite out of the milkweed leaf. It pauses. It sheds the skin which has become too tight for it. Now it goes back to eating.

It is later now, and the caterpillar has shed its skin several times and has reached full growth. It is fat and soft. It is bigger now, we can watch it take big bites from the leaf. It moves its head up and down the edge of the leaf, taking big bites. The leaf is disappearing right in front of our eyes!

The caterpillar is a different color now. It has black and yellow stripes around its green body. Ask the caterpillar why it has such bright stripes. He is telling you. He says, "I have a very bitter taste. By making bright stripes, birds will recognize me and avoid eating me. They hate my bitter taste."

You reach over and pick up the caterpillar. You see that near the front end are six normal-looking eyes. That is the number of legs of a butterfly. At the end are a row of fleshy stumps to clasp the leaf and give balance.

It's later now. The caterpillar looks sick. It has become sluggish. It won't eat. On its skin a tough membrane is forming. It is later yet. The caterpillar has found a place on a leaf. From a special gland at his rear end, a little gluey substance is secreted. We look very carefully at the gluey substance and find that it is liquid silk! Now the caterpillar uses that glue to attach himself. As it dries he is glued to the leaf!

Now he lets go! His legs and head hang down. Now the final step. The skin of the caterpillar splits. It is very thin and light. It drops to the ground. Only a moment before there was a caterpillar, now there is a chrysalis. It is pale and luminous. It is the color of the leaf. It has a row of small gilded dots the color of gold leaf.

Open your eyes. I want you to draw something you remember from what you have just seen.

Suggested follow-up activity:

Class, in our next session we will watch another miracle of nature. We will see the yellow-brown developing wings form. Later we will see a feeble butterfly emerge with its wings all crumpled. We will watch yet another miracle as a beautiful Monarch takes form and then takes flight!

Relax...Look at your fingertip...close your eyes...

Imagine you are shrinking...smaller and smaller...You are so small you disappear under the skin of your own fingertip. Before you, you see a blood vessel...you decide to make yourself smaller. You look at your watch, push start, and poke inside the vessel.

Suddenly you're rushed away in what seems to be a pipeline...It's like a flowing stream...You swim as quickly as possible to a passing red blood cell... You grab ahold, climb up and sit on top of it. Watch out! This red rubber saucer plays bumper cars with all the other red and white blood cells around it. CRASH!! You just ran into a platelet. You hold on tight to the sides of the red blood cell as you quickly pass your elbow, then up to your shoulder and then suddenly you fall down a swift waterfall and tumble into a large chamber on the right side of your heart. As you look around you notice you're in the right atrium and your red blood cell looks "exhausted."

Before you know it, you are swept downward. Two large valves close above you with a "thump." As you look around on your spinning cell, you notice you are

now inside the second chamber of the heart: the right ventricle. Then "THUD!" You're twirling, you're swirling...you're being pushed forward into the lungs! You're blasted out of the heart into the pulmonary artery.

It's peaceful in the lungs. You jump off your red blood cell and watch it get redder and redder as it refuels with new oxygen. Quickly you jump on before it takes off, rip-roaring. You both rush through the pulmonary veins into the third chamber of the heart.

As you enter the left atrium, or third chamber of your heart, you hear a THUD! A valve opens and you are rushed down into the left ventricle. It looks as though you're trapped...suddenly two large valves open and with a big burst you are pushed out of the heart through the aorta. Wow! What a ride you've had!

You now find yourself floating through a yellowish fluid called plasma.You see water, proteins, and salts all around you. The white blood cells are like sharks gobbling up the diseased germs all around them.

Within seconds everything around you seems to be closing in on you. As you enter a capillary, the red blood cells line up in single-file order and slow down. Now is your chance. You stand on top of your blood cell and dive back through the vessel and out of your skin. You're thinking what a day you've had! What an experience!

As you glance at your watch you cannot believe your eyes. The whole voyage took 1 minute!

Close your eyes...Relax...Picture yourself looking back in time...

Think back to a great day you enjoyed. Where are you? What are you doing? Are there other people around you? Who are they?

You are happy...What is making you so happy? Listen...there are sounds around you...what are the sounds you are hearing?

Now open your eyes. Tell us about your "enjoyable day" and why that day is enjoyable to you.

Someone Special

Sit up...Relax...Close your eyes...

Think of an important person in your life. It could be someone you see every day, or someone you haven't seen for a long time. Picture the two of you together... What are you doing? What is the name of your special person? Take a step back and look at your special person...Is your special person looking at you? What are they feeling? How can you tell? Take a closer look at him or her. How is your special person dressed?

You are now off to do something together...Where are you going? Conversations come easy for the two of you...Listen...what are you talking about? You get to your destination...Where are you? The two of you are interacting...What are you doing?

Now open your eyes. Tell us about your "someone special" and why that person is special to you.

Close your eyes...Relax...Picture what I say and let yourself go with what you see, feel, and think.

You stand inside the entrance to your room. You don't move. You look to the left. Your eyes settle on something. Still not moving, a thought comes to mind about that thing.

Now you let that thought go and visually scan the room. Certain colors catch your eyes. The colors create a feeling. You let yourself have that feeling...

Now you see something interesting in the room. You walk to it. Pick it up. How does it feel? Is it heavy or light? That item says something important about you. What is it saying? Keep that thought...

Slowly you open your eyes...If someone walked into your room and did not know you, what would they learn about you from their visit?

Write your answer on the worksheet "My Room." Include details of several things the visitor would see.

BE KIND 2 KIDS
Name:
my dad
my older brother
my older sister
my mom
ring bell
to enter
PUSH!
my ROOM
do not enter! that means u!!
4th grade
3rd grade
2nd grade
1st grade
emergency entrance
4 peoples in my club only!

Class, I want you all to sit straight in your chairs. Take a deep breath. Let it all out. Now close your eyes. With your eyes shut, look at the backs of your eyelids and you will see everything I say, just like a movie!

You are going to see a circus! First, you are standing in line outside the big circus tents. There is sawdust on the ground, and a clown blowing long skinny balloons. Look at the clown blowing balloons. The clown twists the balloons to make animals. Now the clown is coming to you. The clown bends down and asks you what color balloon you would like. Without talking out loud, just in your movie, tell him. Now he is asking you what kind of balloon animal you would like. Tell him what kind of animal you want. Now the clown is blowing up a long skinny balloon for you. The clown ties it off at the end so the air can't come out. The clown twists the balloon and makes your animal. He hands it to you and stands up. You say, "thank you!"

Now you look up and see three huge tents. You go into the tents and sit down on a bench. The show is about to start. The Ringmaster steps inside the middle wooden ring and picks up a microphone. In a loud, deep voice, he says, "Ladies, gentlemen, and children, welcome to the circus, the show is about to **begin!**"

Just then, a man leads out three giant elephants. The elephants have skin which is grey, loose, and wrinkly. The elephants walk in a line, using their trunks to hold the tail of the one in front of them. On the back of each elephant is a lady in a pretty, shiny suit. The ladies are all dressed the same. Look carefully and you will see their headpieces. Remember the color of their suits and the design of their headpieces. Now the elephants all stand on their back legs. The ladies move up on the elephants' heads so they don't fall off! Everyone claps!

Next, the Ringmaster calls out, "Ladies, Gentlemen, and Children, look up! You are about to see the daring trapeze family." You look up, and on a very high platform you see a man and a girl. On another platform on the other side of the circus tent is a woman and a boy. They are all dressed in tight, shiny clothes. The woman is holding a bar. The woman swings off the platform holding the bar. Up and back she pumps her legs, like on a swing, to fly faster and faster. Higher and higher. Now she swings up to the boy. He grabs her feet. They swing together. Now the man jumps off the platform, holding the bar. When he swings back up, the girl grabs his feet. The man and girl are swinging toward the woman and the boy. Watch them swing. When they get close, the boy and girl each jump forward and trade places! Now the girl is swinging with the woman and the boy is swinging with the man. Everyone claps!

There is noise all around you! You look around the big circus tent. You see flags of different colors...people holding pink cotton candy...a lion-tamer with a whip and a lion...
bareback riders on horses...
everyone laughing or clapping. Take a moment, keep your eyes shut. What else can you see?

Now open your eyes, turn to your partner, and tell your partner everything you saw: the color of your balloon, your balloon animal, the Ladies on the elephants...What else could you see...

Teams solve each problem using the unique clues provided by each teammate.

Multiple Intelligences

★★ Verbal/Linguistic
★★★ Logical/Mathematical
★★★ Visual/Spatial
Musical/Rhythmic
★ Bodily/Kinesthetic
Naturalist
★★ Interpersonal
Intrapersonal

Set up
Teacher prepares clue cards (minimum one per student) and game board, if necessary.
Steps
1. Clue cards are dealt out randomly, as evenly as possible to teammates.
2. Student one reads one of his/her cards, explains the implication of the clue, and carries out that clue.
3. Teammates check, then praise or coach.
4. Student Two reads one of his/her cards, explains, and carries out the clue.
5. Teammates check, then praise or coach.
6. Steps two and three are carried out for each teammate in turn until all clues have been shared and performed.
7. When finished, teammates check their solution and celebrate.

The clowns are always up to mischief! When the show begins in the big top, it seems like one clown is always missing.

First exposure to simple logic problems may require a highly structured, teacher-directed model. Through modeling, discussions, and careful questioning on the part of the teacher, students make observations to solve the problem of "The Lost Clown."

As students read their **assigned** clues **in order** and **explain** the information provided, they place markers or beans on top of clowns that are eliminated until only the right clown remains.

Answers on page 254

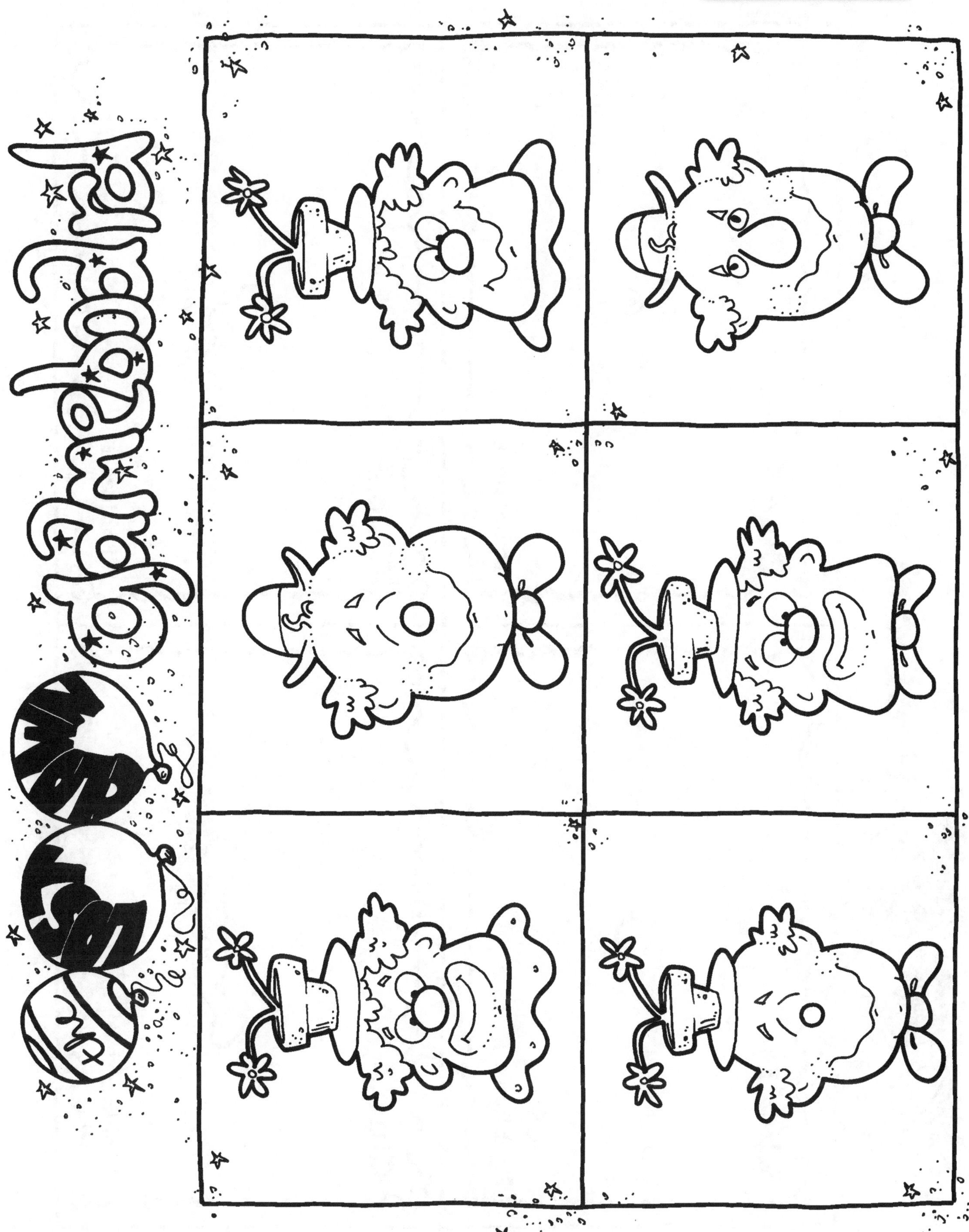

Problem I

cut out cards

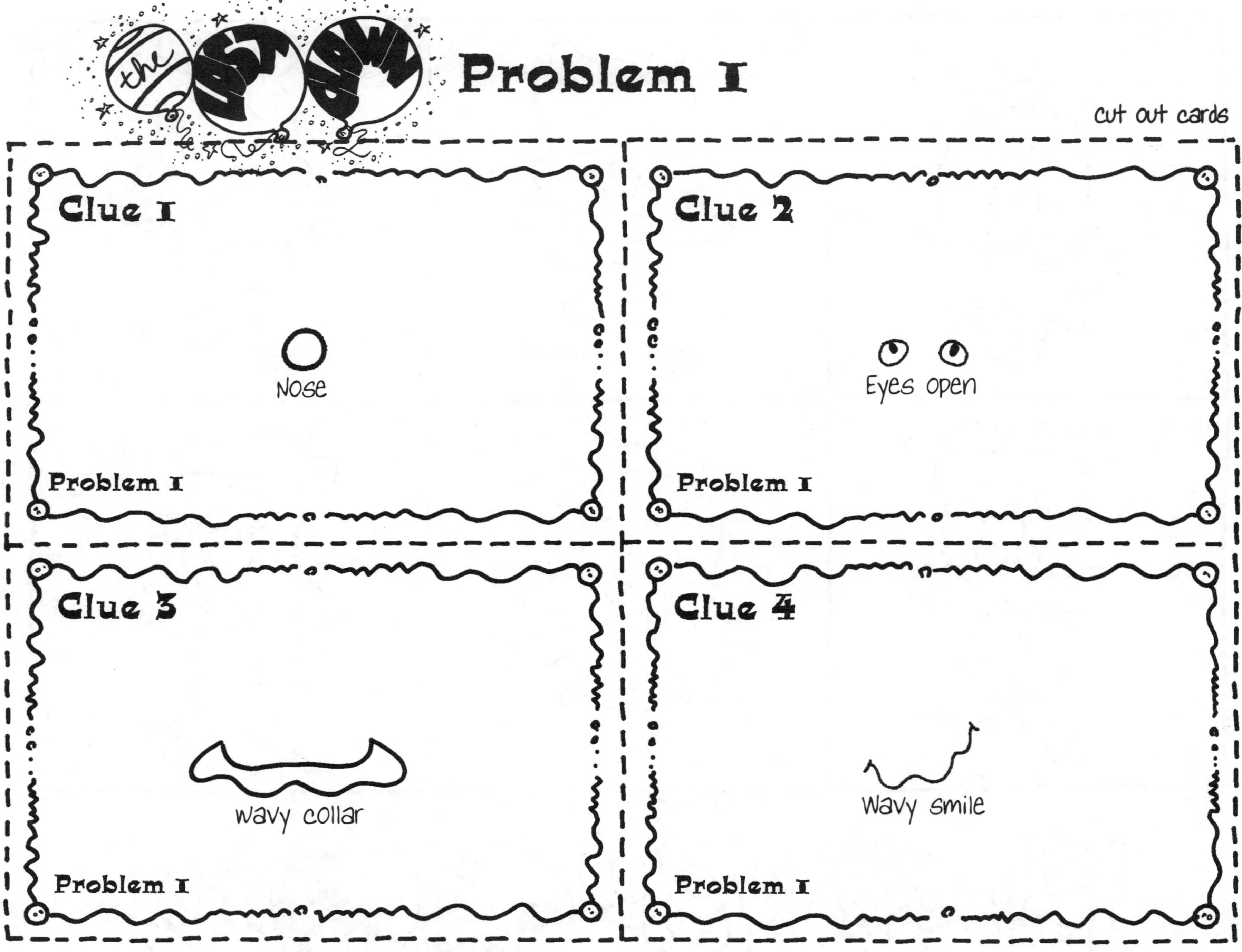

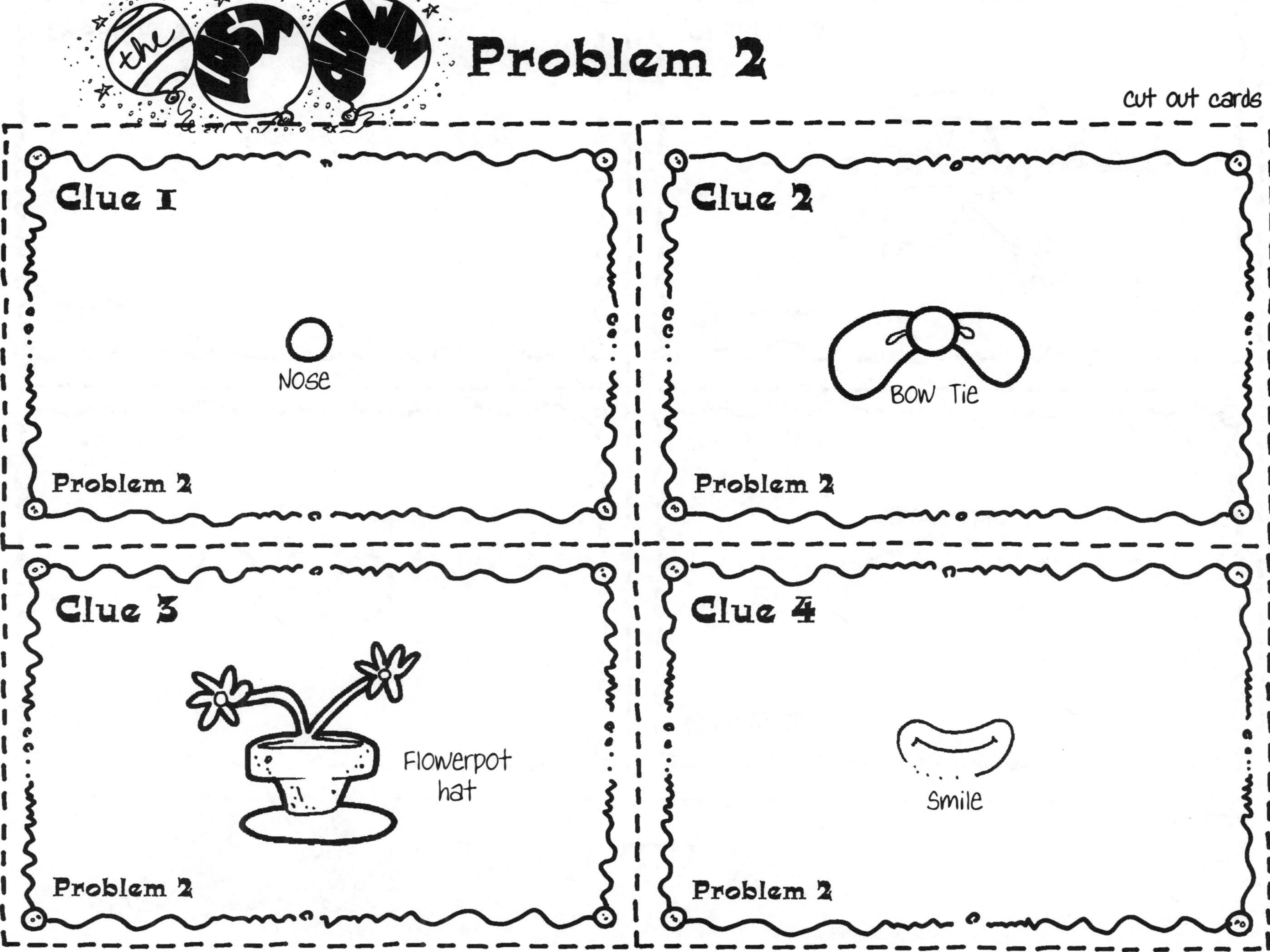
Problem 2
cut out cards
Clue 1
Nose
Problem 2
Clue 2
Bow Tie
Problem 2
Clue 3
Flowerpot hat
Problem 2
Clue 4
Smile
Problem 2

Problem 3

cut out cards

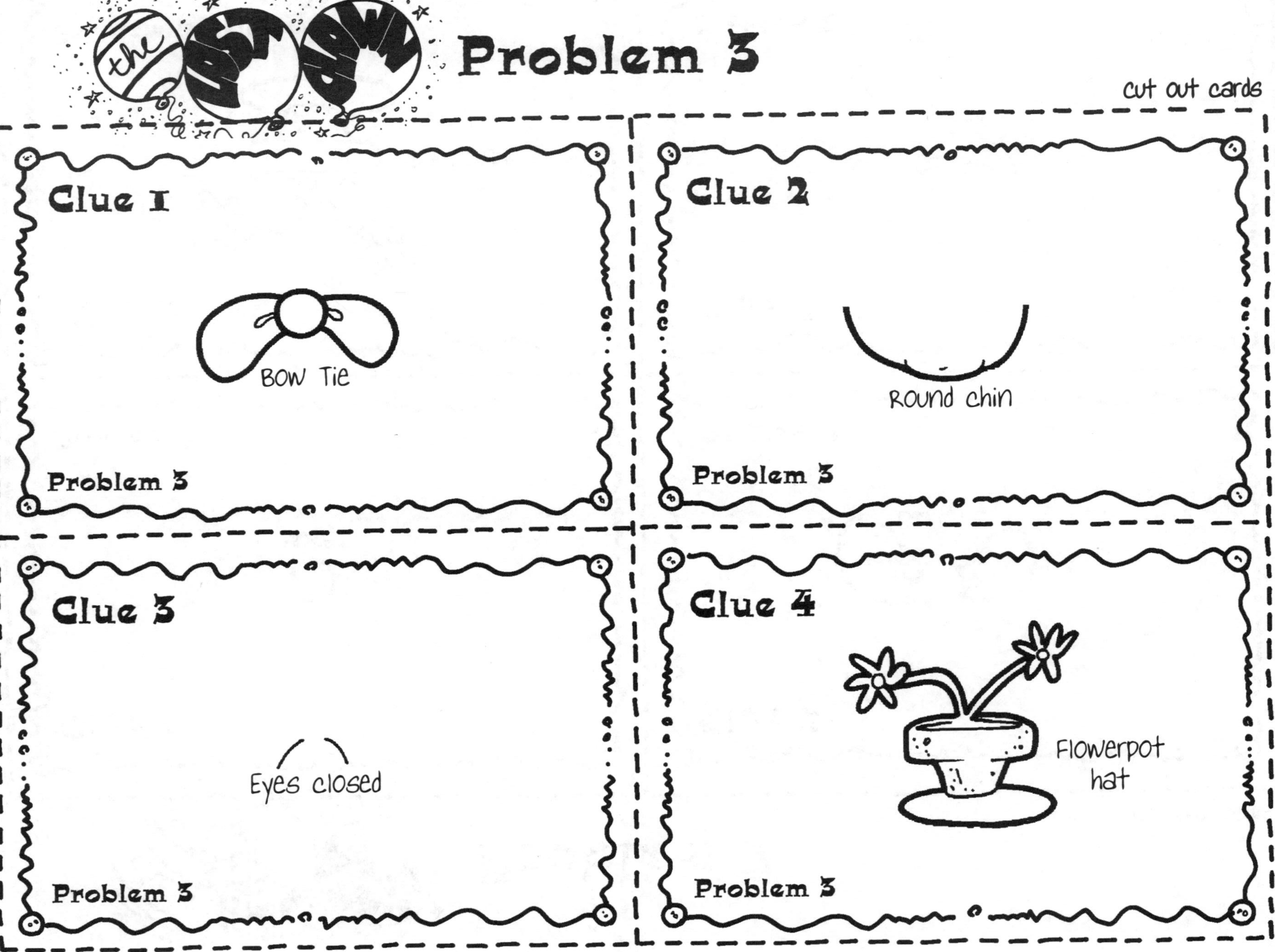

The Wise Old Owl has lost his memory and his clue cards!

Your team has just found the clue cards. As a team, can you help the wise old owl put his shapes in order for each problem? First pass out the shapes (one shape for each teammember). Second, pass out the Problem Clue Cards. Play Jigsaw Problem Solving!

Problem 1

First	Second	Third	Fourth

Problem 2

First	Second	Third	Fourth

Problem 3

First	Second	Third	Fourth

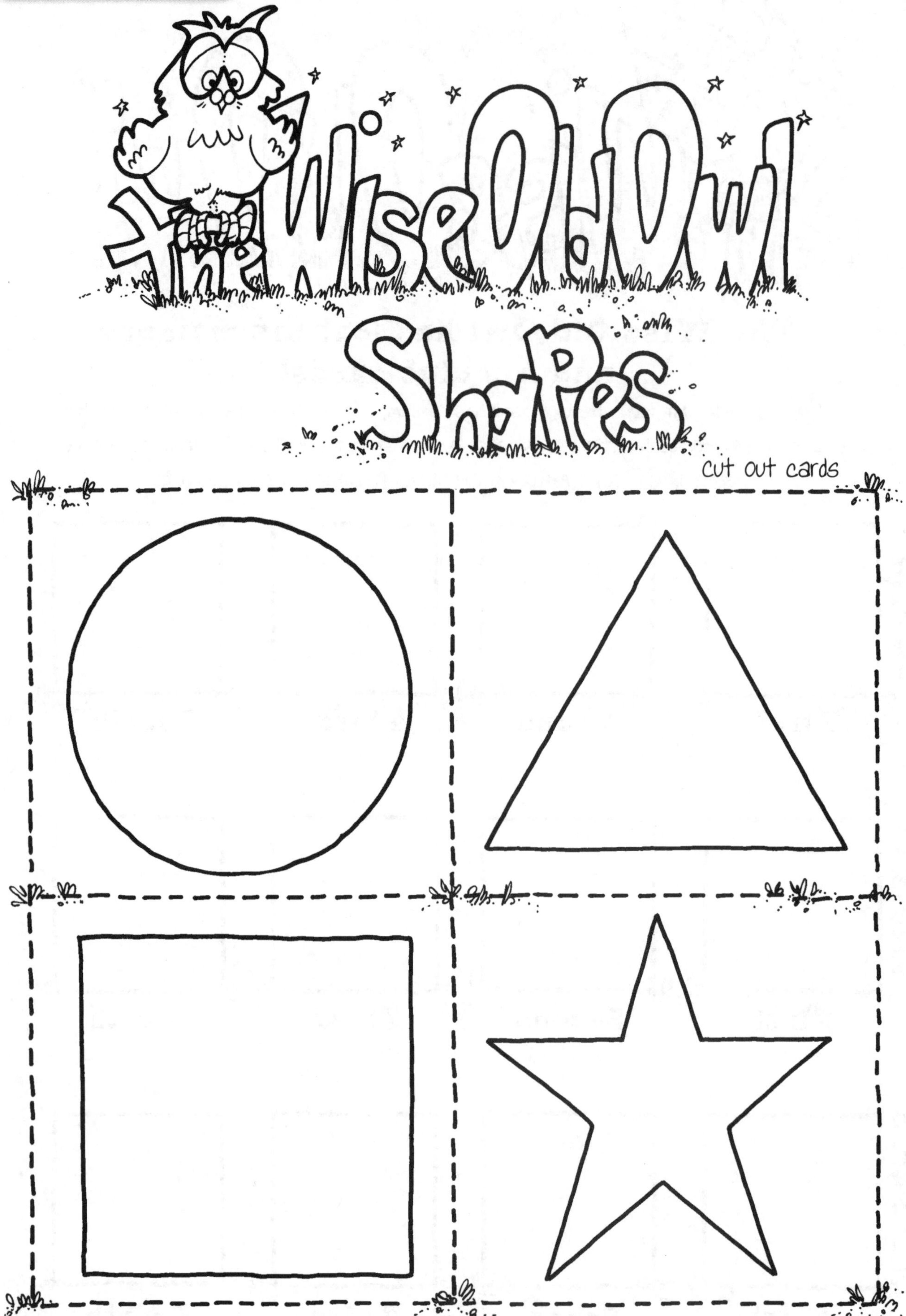
The Wise Old Owl
Shapes
cut out cards

The Wise Old Owl

Problem I

cut out cards

Clue I

The triangle is not first.

Problem I

Clue 2

The circle is between the star and the square.

Problem I

Clue 3

The star is between the triangle and the circle.

Problem I

Clue 4

The circle is ahead of the star.

Problem I

The Wise Old Owl

Problem 2

cut out cards

Clue 1

The triangle is not last.

Problem 2

Clue 2

The square is not between the star and the circle.

Problem 2

Clue 3

The star is between the triangle and the square.

Problem 2

Clue 4

The circle is in front of the triangle.

Problem 2

The Wise Old Owl

Problem 3

cut out cards

Clue 1	Clue 2
The circle is somewhere behind the star.	The square is in front of the triangle.
Problem 3	Problem 3

Clue 3	Clue 4
The first shape is not the square.	The shape directly behind the star is not the circle.
Problem 3	Problem 3

Peter Penguin's Problems

Peter Penguin is having trouble constructing an igloo. Can you help him by using sugar cubes?

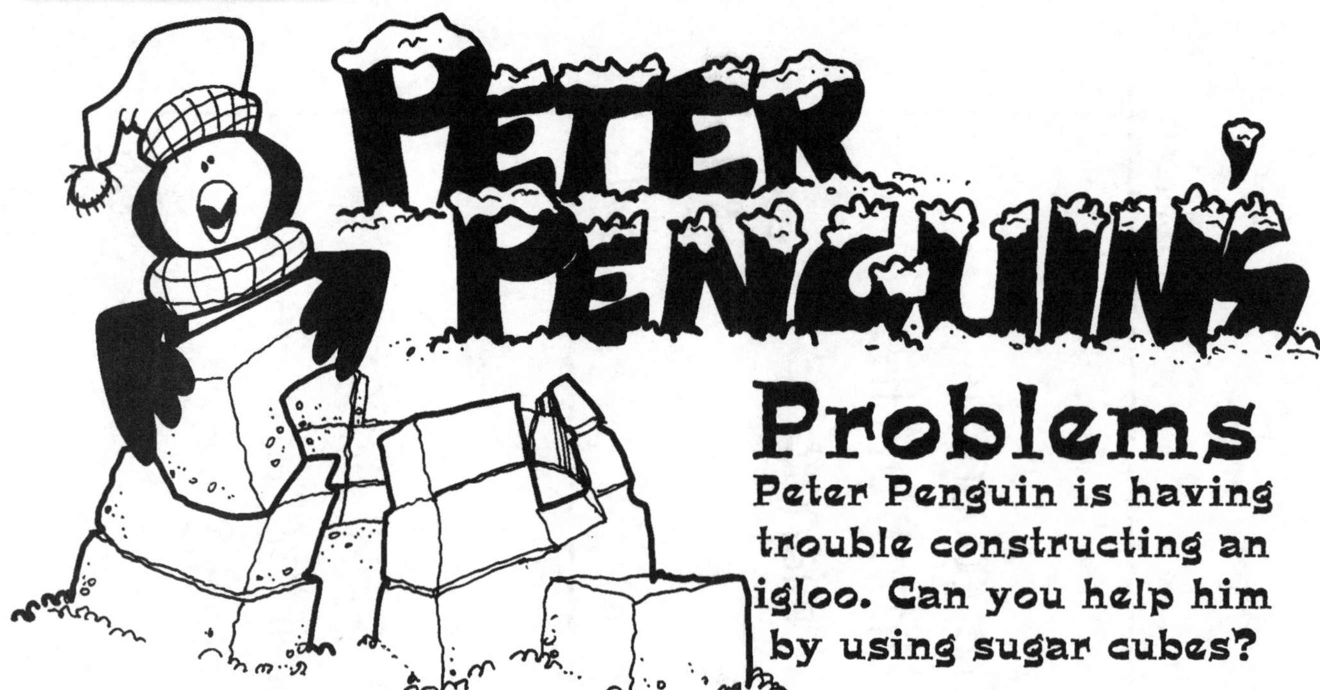

Pass out clue cards to each teammember. Each person must solve the problem by moving around the cubes on the worksheet. Record your answer using a "Rotating Recorder." (Note: The edge of one block equals one unit in length.)

Answer Sheet

Draw the back view.

Problem 1

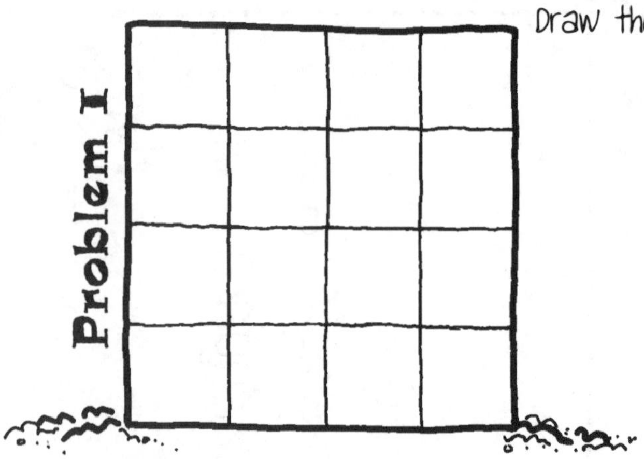

Problem 2

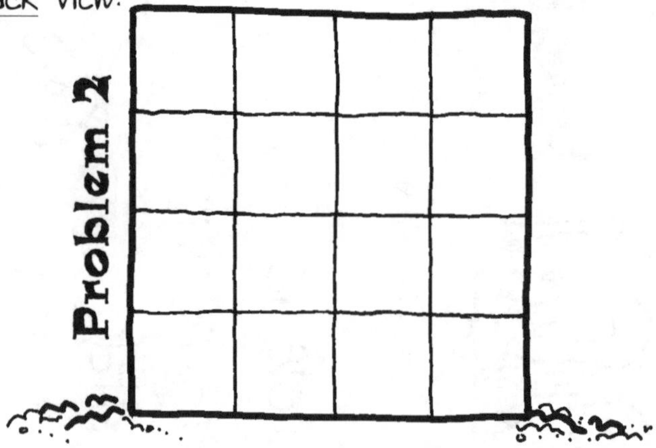

Problem 3

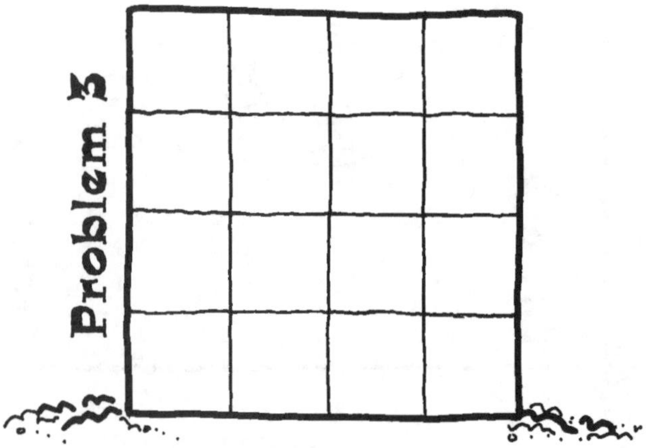

Problem 4

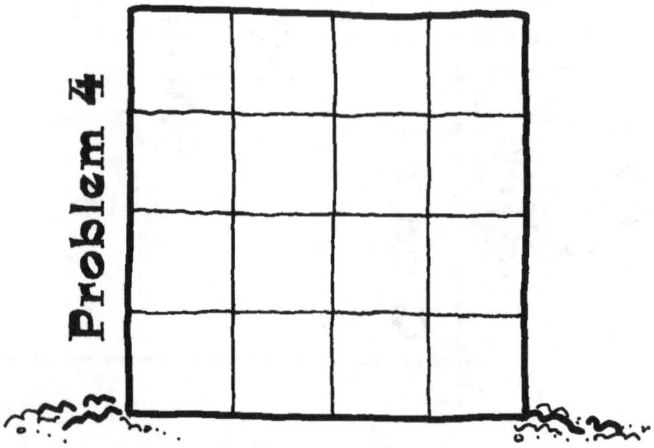

Peter Penguin's Workboard

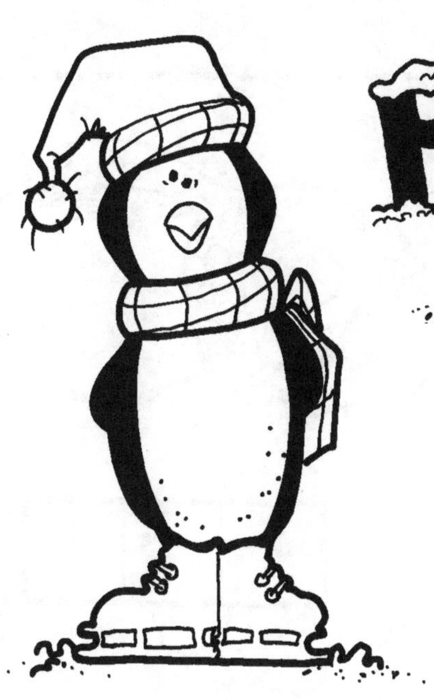

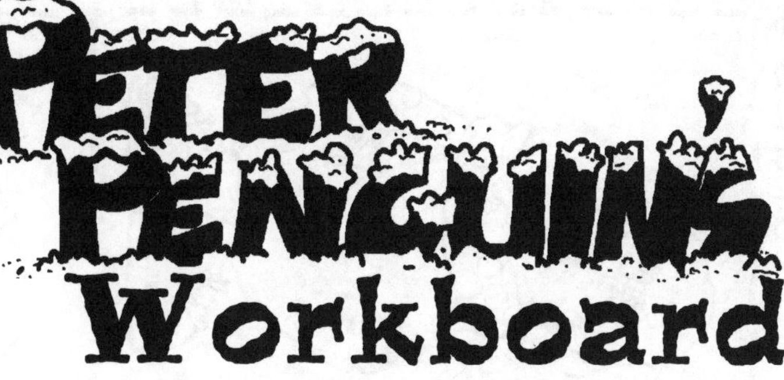

one per team

Remember to look at the problem at direct eye level!

Back view

Left view

Right view

Front view

Peter Penguin's Problem 1
cut out cards
Clue 1
Top view
Problem 1
Clue 2
Left view
Problem 1
Clue 3
Front view
Problem 1
Clue 4
Right view
Problem 1

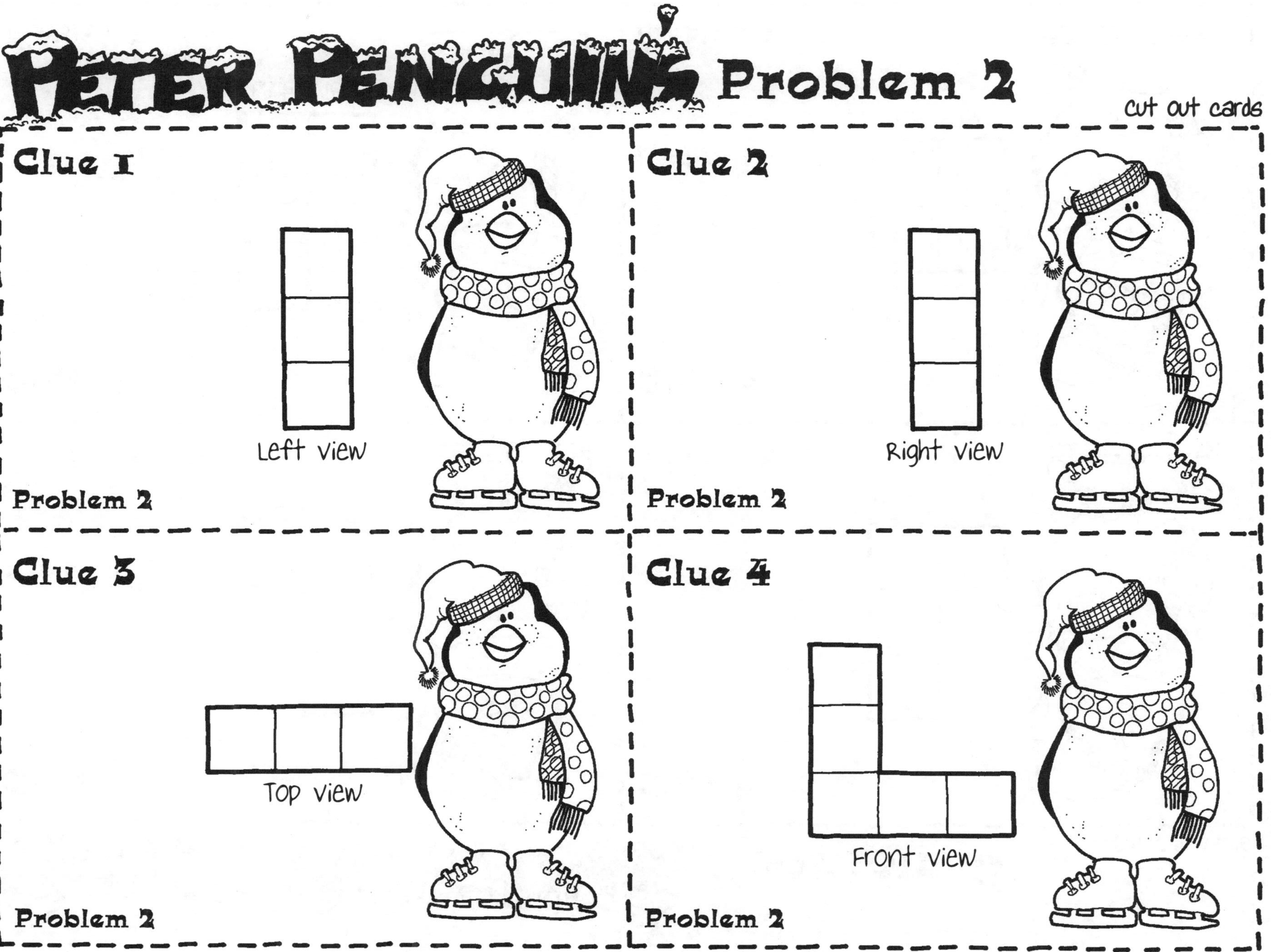
Peter Penguin's Problem 2
cut out cards
Clue 1
Left view
Problem 2
Clue 2
Right view
Problem 2
Clue 3
Top view
Problem 2
Clue 4
Front view
Problem 2

Peter Penguin's Problem 3
cut out cards
Clue 1
Right view
Problem 3
Clue 2
Front view
Problem 3
Clue 3
Left view
Problem 3
Clue 4
Top view
Problem 3

Peter Penguin's Problem 4
cut out cards
Clue 1
Front view
Problem 4
Clue 2
Top view
Problem 4
Clue 3
Right view
Problem 4
Clue 4
Left view
Problem 4

Teammates use clues, student picture cards, and higher-order thinking skills to solve this "Around the World" logic problem.

Students must be arranged in order, holding hands and facing inward, around the world. Words such as **between, clockwise, right, left,** and **across** are used and interpreted by each team.

Again, it is important to remember that each team must read their clues in order. Each clue needs to be studied and explained with care, then all possible inferences should be drawn. The first explainer is always the teammember who was responsible for reading that specific clue. After the explainer finishes, teammembers discuss.

Answers on page 256

Step 1:

Cut out and pass out two students per person. Remember, only you can touch your students if they need to move.

Step 2:

- Pass out two clues per person. Start with clue number one.
- You and only you may read your clue and explain what to do.
- Teammates will agree or disagree and explain their reasoning.

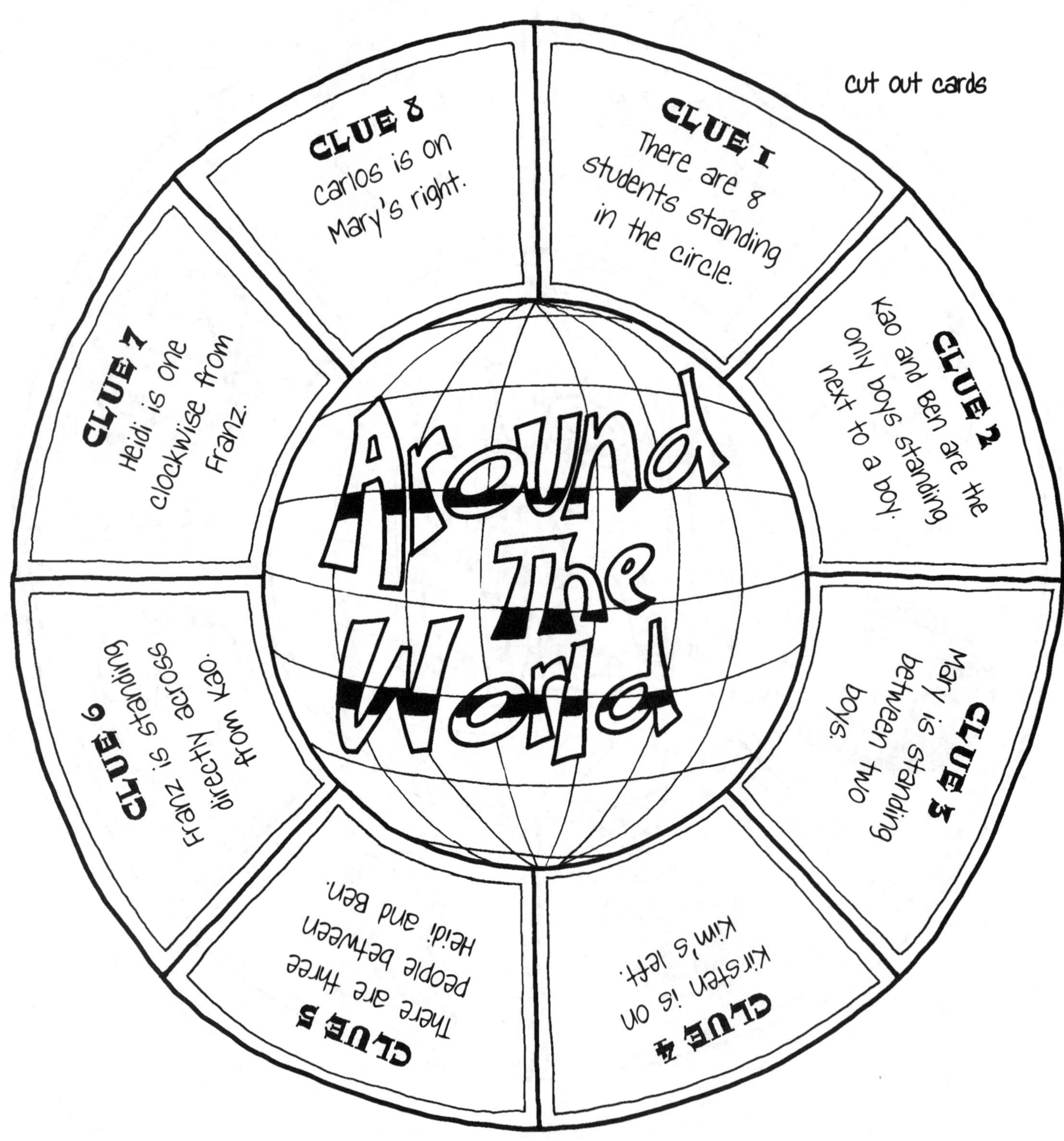

Skiing
Lake Tahoe
Laurie wants to leave her house in Homewood and ski Incline Village!
Tahoe City
Bridge
Bridge
South Shore
Incline Village
Homewood
16
16
14
Your team must figure out the shortest way to get to Incline Village.
Cut up and divide clue cards evenly among your teammates.
Solve the problem using this map of the lake as a workboard.

cut out cards

Lake Tahoe

Here is a sign in Incline Village, showing

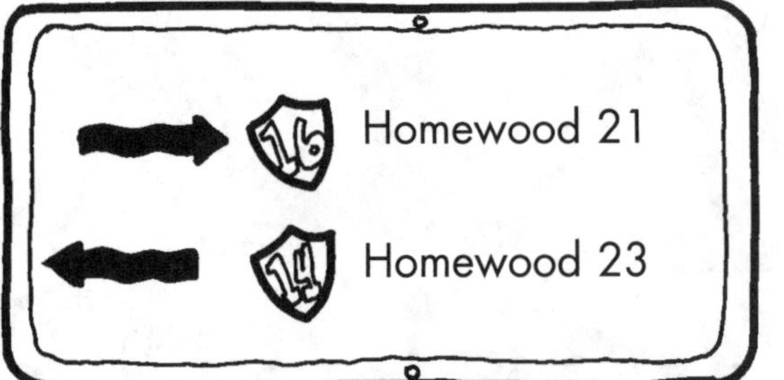

the distances along two different highways to Homewood. Two highways connect Incline Village to Homewood. Highway 16 winds along the north shore of the lake, while Highway 14 winds along the south shore. Record what you know.

Lake Tahoe

Here is a sign in Emeral Bay in front

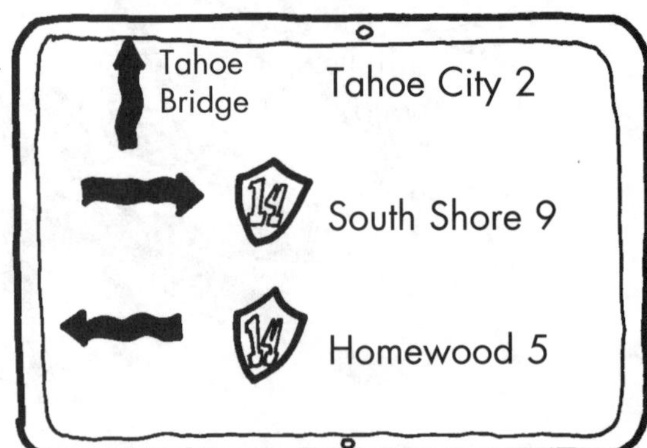

of Tahoe Bridge. All seven towns on the shores of Lake Tahoe are connected by bridges and winding highways. Record mileage on the map.

Clue 3

Lake Tahoe

Here is a sign in Carnelian Bay.

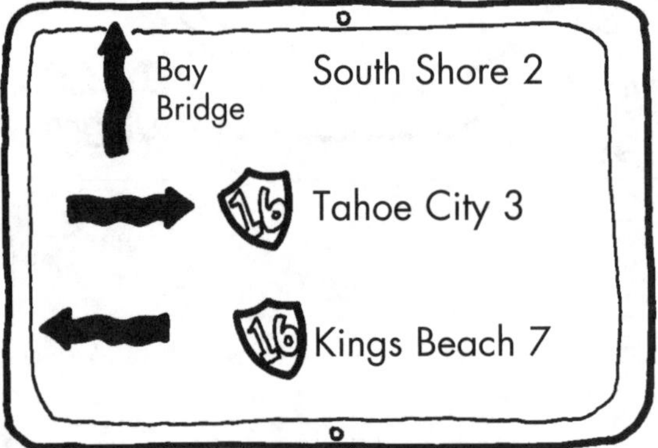

Lake Tahoe is long and thin, winding more or less east and west. It has two bridges: the Bay Bridge and the Tahoe Bridge.

Lake Tahoe

In this problem, you and your group must

find the shortest route from Homewood to Incline Village. This sign is along Highway 16 in Kings Beach.

It's not as easy as you think!

Adapted from: United We Solve

Historical
MOMENTS
There are three ways to play!
Most Difficult: Provide students with only the Jigsaw Problem Solving clue cards. They discover the sequence and date of each event, drawing their own timeline.
Easier: Provide students with the Jigsaw Problem Solving clue cards and the "Fill in the Date" cards. Their job: They fill in their answers on the cards.
Easiest: Provide students with the Jigsaw Problem Solving Cards, the Historic Moments Timeline, and the "Fill in the Date" cards. Students manipulate and write dates on the "Fill in the Date" cards. When finished, students fill in the Historical Timeline.
Answers on page 257

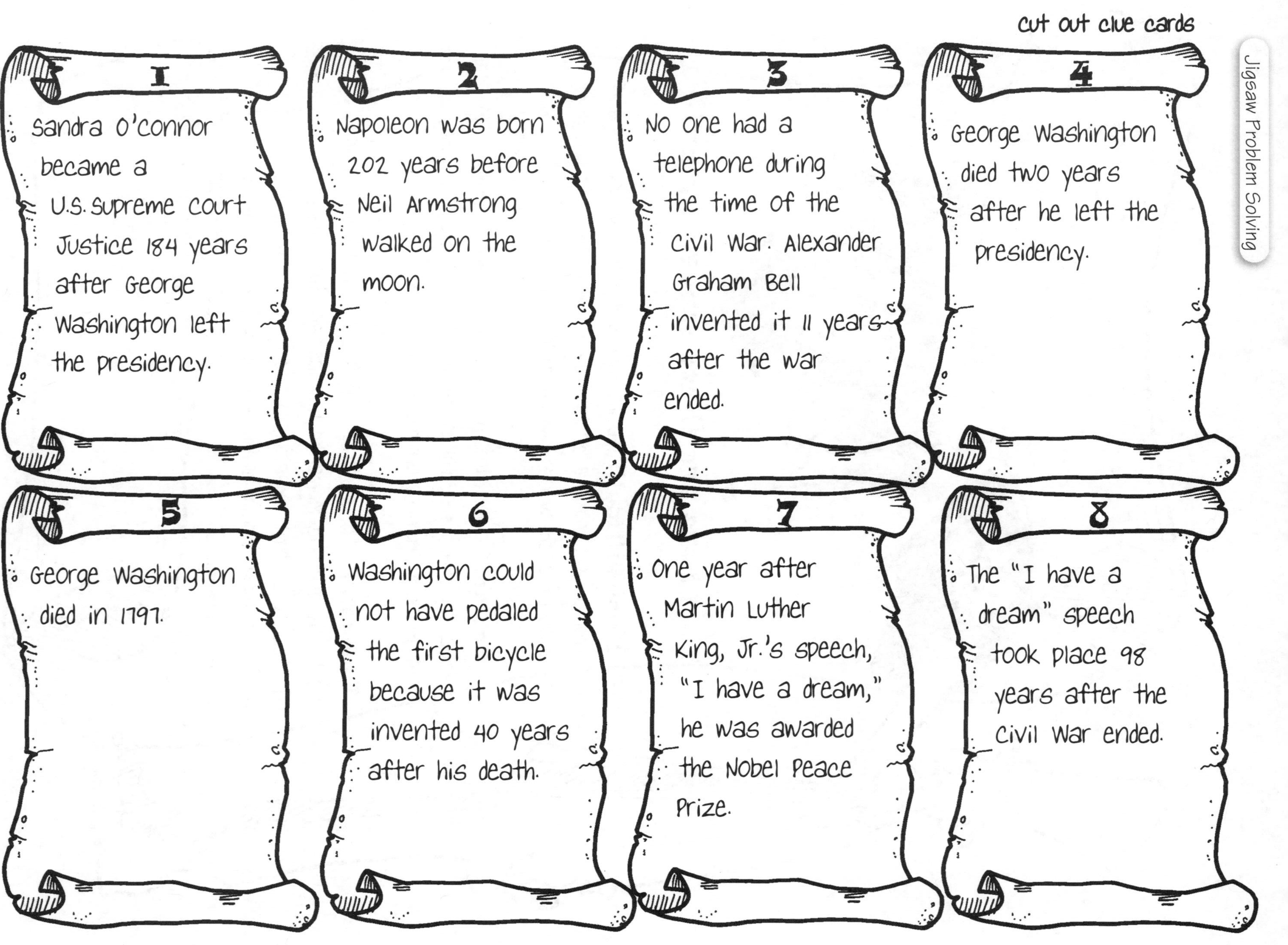
cut out clue cards
1
Sandra O'Connor became a U.S. Supreme Court Justice 184 years after George Washington left the presidency.
2
Napoleon was born 202 years before Neil Armstrong walked on the moon.
3
No one had a telephone during the time of the Civil War. Alexander Graham Bell invented it 11 years after the war ended.
4
George Washington died two years after he left the presidency.
5
George Washington died in 1797.
6
Washington could not have pedaled the first bicycle because it was invented 40 years after his death.
7
One year after Martin Luther King, Jr.'s speech, "I have a dream," he was awarded the Nobel Peace Prize.
8
The "I have a dream" speech took place 98 years after the Civil War ended.

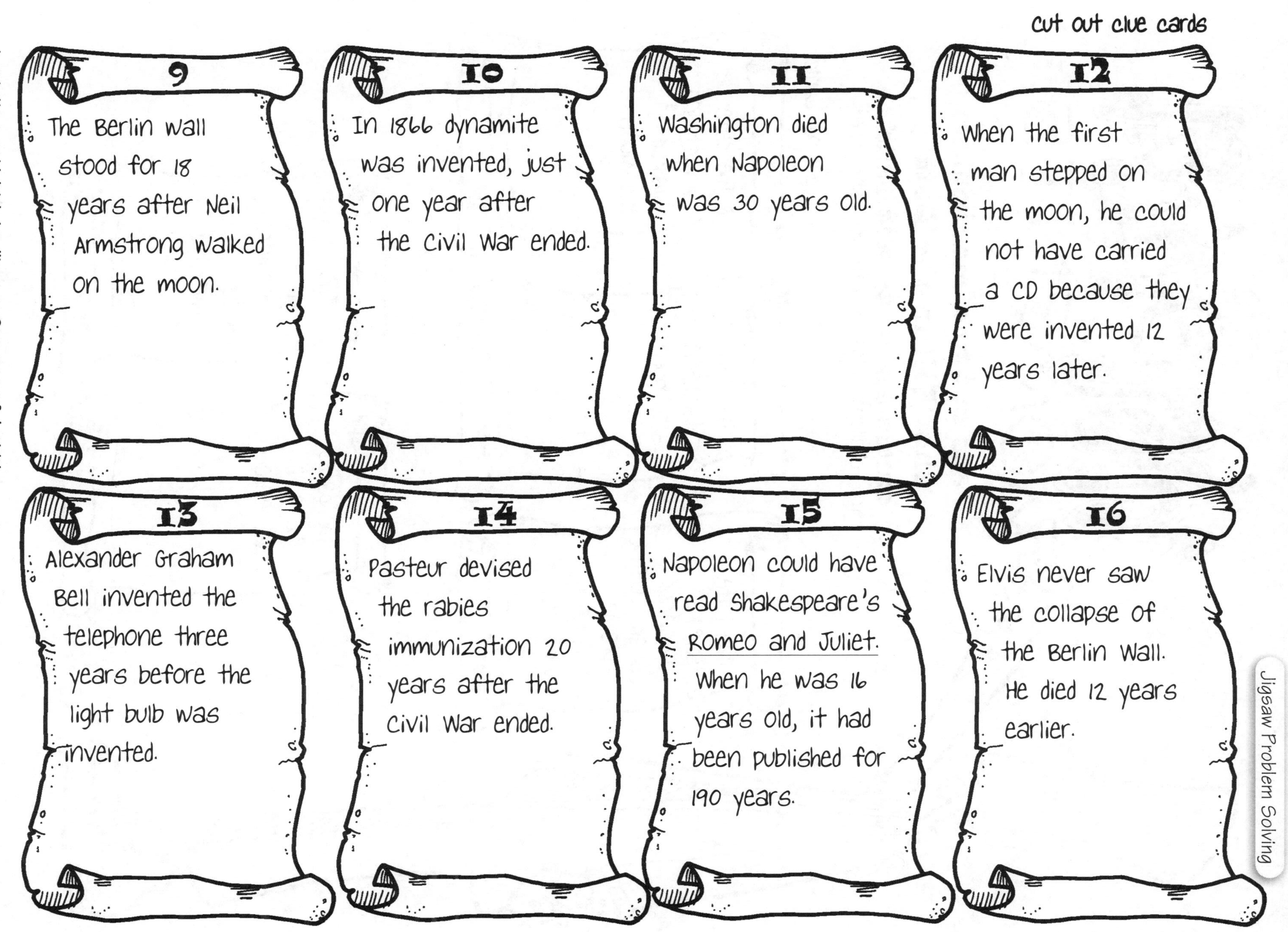
cut out clue cards
9
The Berlin wall stood for 18 years after Neil Armstrong walked on the moon.
10
In 1866 dynamite was invented, just one year after the Civil War ended.
11
Washington died when Napoleon was 30 years old.
12
When the first man stepped on the moon, he could not have carried a CD because they were invented 12 years later.
13
Alexander Graham Bell invented the telephone three years before the light bulb was invented.
14
Pasteur devised the rabies immunization 20 years after the Civil War ended.
15
Napoleon could have read Shakespeare's Romeo and Juliet. When he was 16 years old, it had been published for 190 years.
16
Elvis never saw the collapse of the Berlin Wall. He died 12 years earlier.

historical
MOMENTS
Pass out and manipulate the "Fill in the Date" cards as clues are read.
Your challenge: Find the date for each event.
cut out cards
The date Sandra O'connor became U.S. Supreme Court Justice:
The date Napoleon was born:
The date Neil Armstrong walked on the moon:
The date the Civil War ended:
The date the telephone was invented:

The date Washington left the presidency:
The date the first bicycle was invented:
The date Martin Luther King, Jr. was awarded the Nobel Peace Prize:
The date the Berlin Wall fell:
The date Washington died:
The date the "I Have A Dream" speech took place:
The date dynamite was invented:
The date the CD was invented:
The date the light bulb was invented:
The date Elvis died:
The date the rabies immunization was devised:
The date Romeo and Juliet was published:

historical
MOMENTS
Timeline
Discover and write in the event for each of these important dates.
1593
1767
1795
1797
1837
1865
1866
1876
Line up and tape the back of the second page to this flap

Cut out timeline and tape the flap at the bottom of the first page to the back of this page.

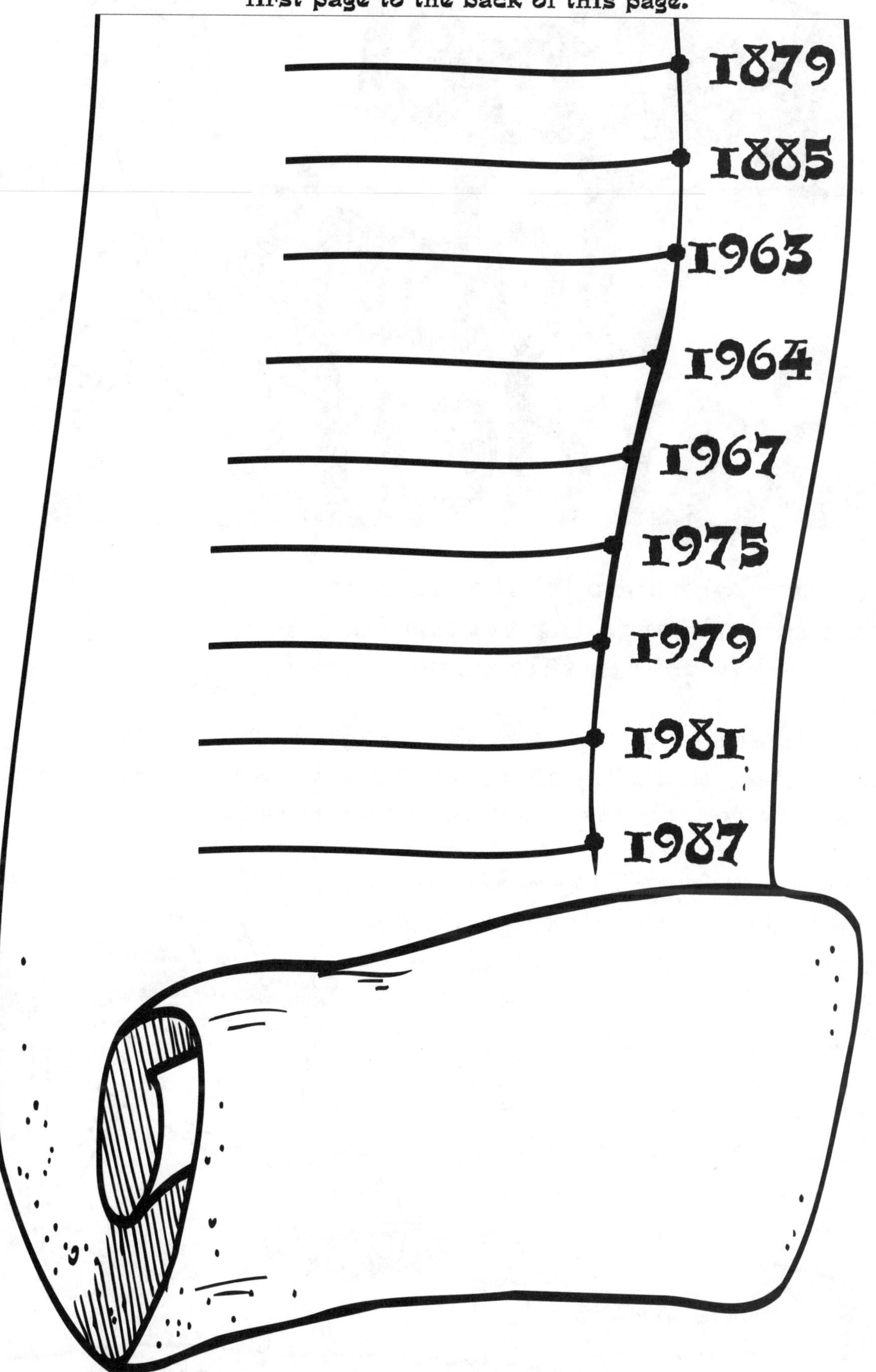

Farmer John's Garden

Farmer John thought it would be fun to rearrange the vegetables in his garden this year!

Nine vegetables are grown in Farmer John's Garden: **Tomatoes, potatoes, string beans, lettuce, beets, celery, carrots, lima beans,** and **corn**. The vegetable garden is arranged three vegetables across and three vegetables down.

There are three separate problems with clue cards. Students cut out the vegetables and move them around on the workboard to assist them in solving the problems. After each clue "seed packet" is read, students share their reasoning with their teammates.

Remember, all the implications of each clue should be discussed and utilized before the next clue is read!

Answers on page 258

Farmer John's Garden

Pass out vegetables. Remember only you can touch your vegetables!

cut out cards

one workboard per team

NORTH

WEST

Farmer John's Garden

EAST

SOUTH

Farmer John's Garden

Problem 1

cut out cards

Farmer John's Garden

Problem 2

cut out cards

Farmer John's Garden

Problem 3

cut out cards

Barnyard Animals

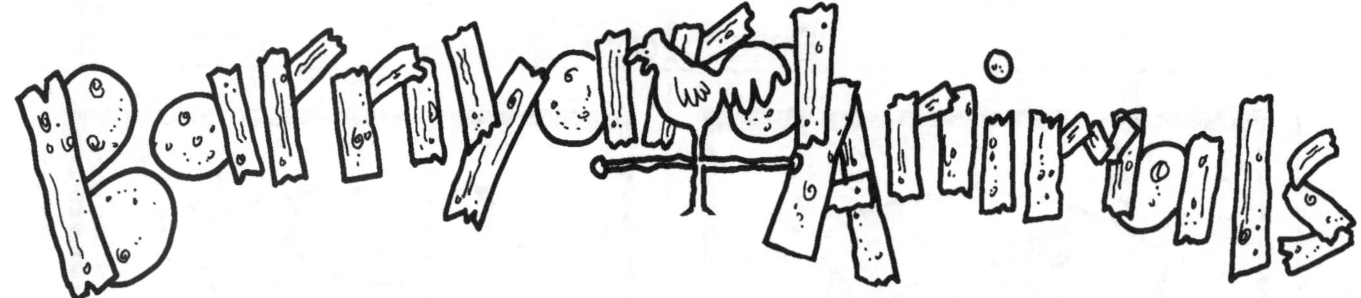

The Barnyard Animals are lost! Can you help them find their way back into the barn?

cut out cards

Step 1:
Pass out cards.

Step 2:
Read the clue cards and, with your knowledge of a compass, figure out where each animal belongs by using the workboard.

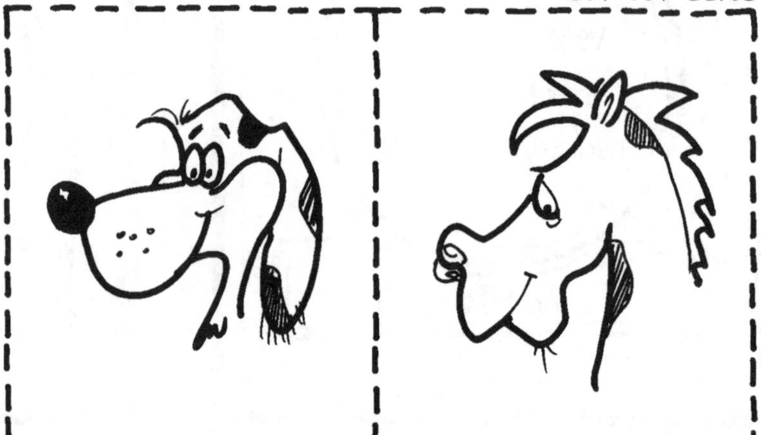

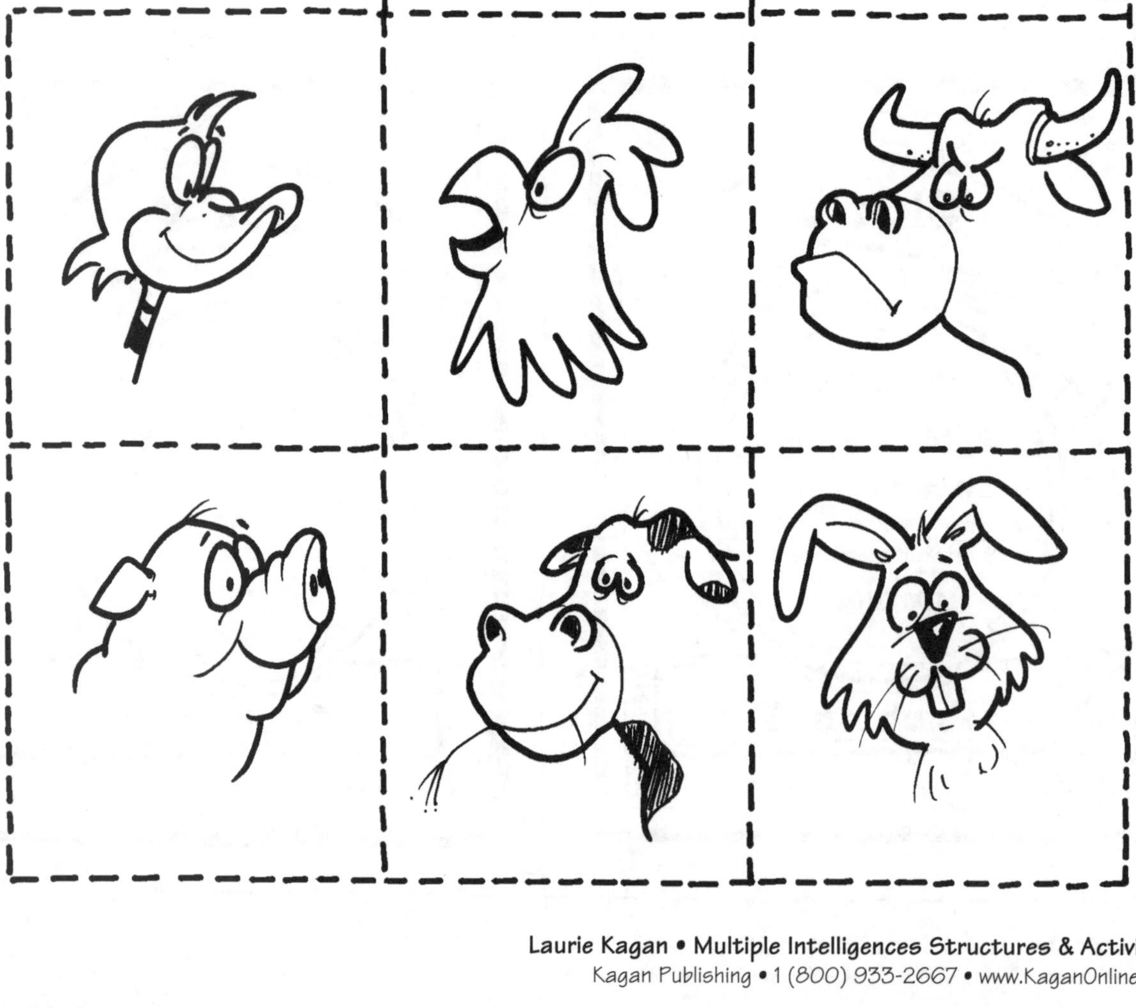

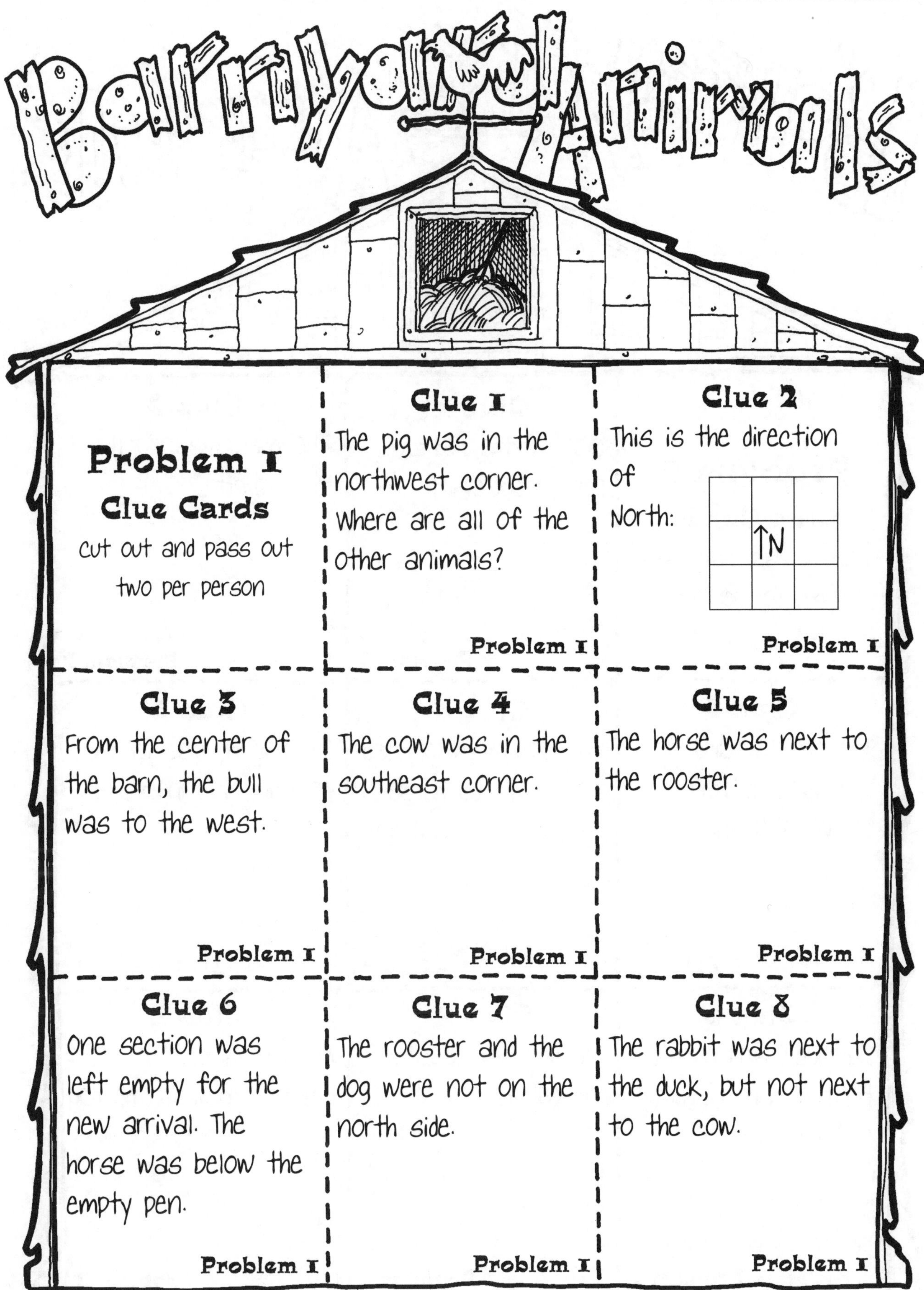
Barnyard Animals

Problem 1
Clue Cards
cut out and pass out
two per person

Clue 1
The pig was in the
northwest corner.
Where are all of the
other animals?
Problem 1

Clue 2
This is the direction
of
North:
↑N
Problem 1

Clue 3
From the center of
the barn, the bull
was to the west.
Problem 1

Clue 4
The cow was in the
southeast corner.
Problem 1

Clue 5
The horse was next to
the rooster.
Problem 1

Clue 6
One section was
left empty for the
new arrival. The
horse was below the
empty pen.
Problem 1

Clue 7
The rooster and the
dog were not on the
north side.
Problem 1

Clue 8
The rabbit was next to
the duck, but not next
to the cow.
Problem 1

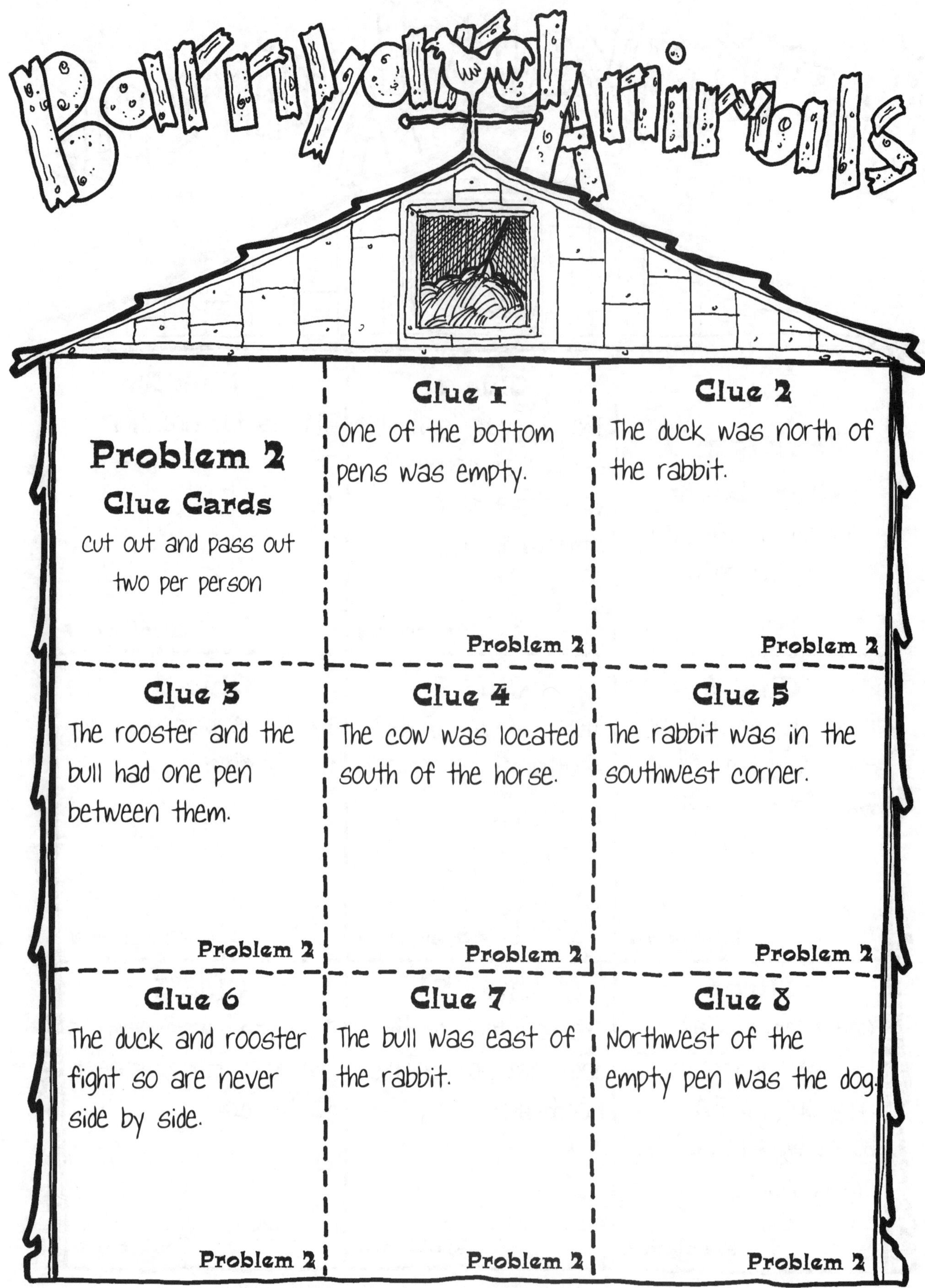
Barnyard Animals

Problem 2
Clue Cards
cut out and pass out two per person

Clue 1
One of the bottom pens was empty.
Problem 2

Clue 2
The duck was north of the rabbit.
Problem 2

Clue 3
The rooster and the bull had one pen between them.
Problem 2

Clue 4
The cow was located south of the horse.
Problem 2

Clue 5
The rabbit was in the southwest corner.
Problem 2

Clue 6
The duck and rooster fight so are never side by side.
Problem 2

Clue 7
The bull was east of the rabbit.
Problem 2

Clue 8
Northwest of the empty pen was the dog.
Problem 2

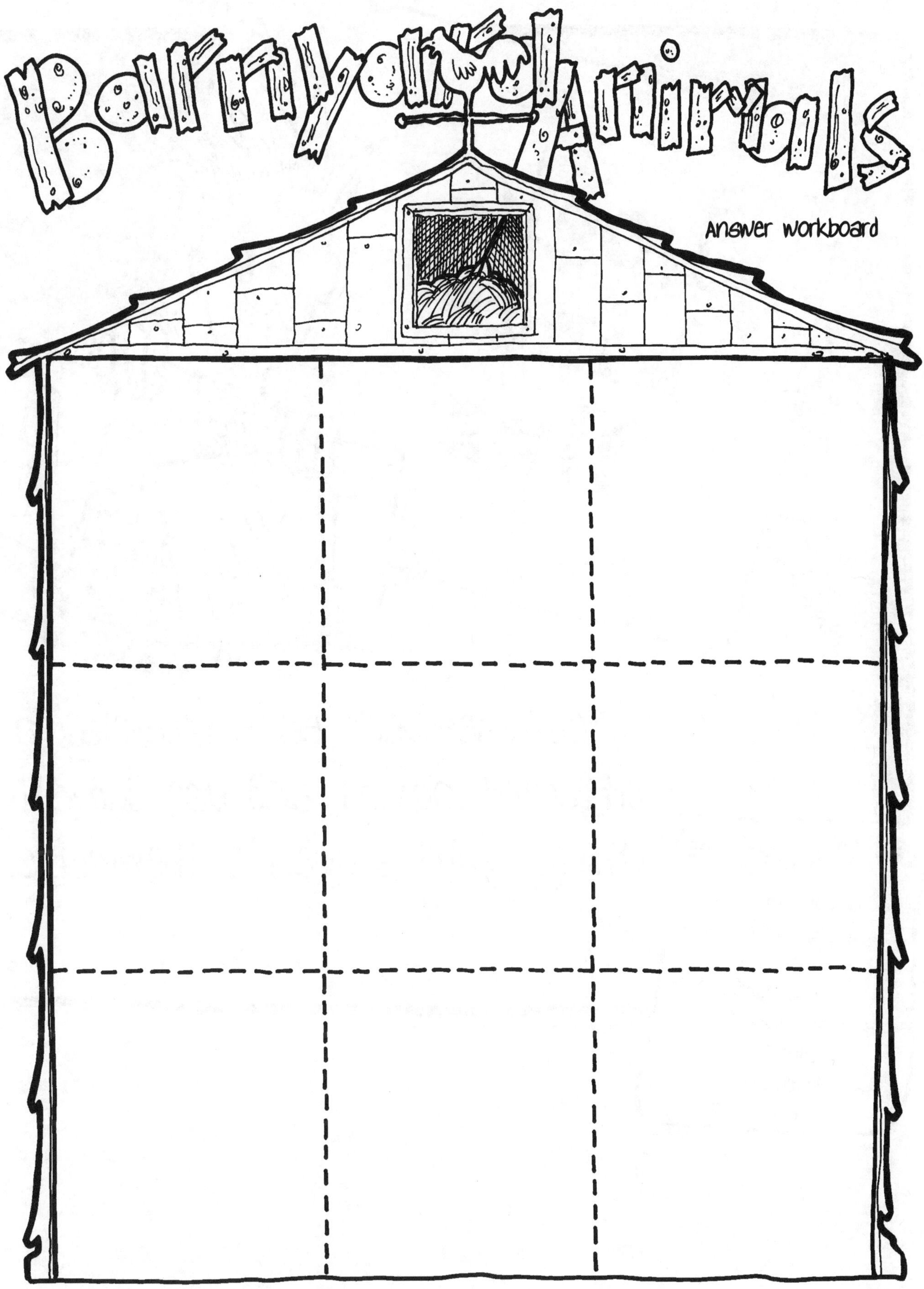
Barnyard Animals
Answer workboard

Teammembers each role-play a different object and use deductive thinking to sequence themselves.

Multiple Intelligences

- ★★ Verbal/Linguistic
- ★★★ Logical/Mathematical
- ★★ Visual/Spatial
- Musical/Rhythmic
- ★★ Bodily/Kinesthetic
- ★ Naturalist
- ★★★ Interpersonal
- Intrapersonal

Set-up

Each team receives four item cards.

Steps

1. Teammates stand shoulder-to-shoulder, each holding an item card.
2. The teacher reads the first clue to problem one.
3. The student mentioned in the clue describes how he/she will line up based on the clue. He/she checks with teammates for agreement. If students disagree, they discuss why. Note: If more than one teammate is mentioned in a clue, they each describe their reasoning and check with teammates for agreement.
4. The student physically moves to his/her place in the team line up.
5. After the teacher reads each clue, students repeat steps 3 and 4.
6. When all clues have been read and acted on, the teacher calls on one team to describe their order and share their logic.
7. The team selected responds.
8. The teacher either congratulates the team or provides correction opportunity. Other teams listen and either celebrate or correct their positions.
9. The process is repeated for the next problem.

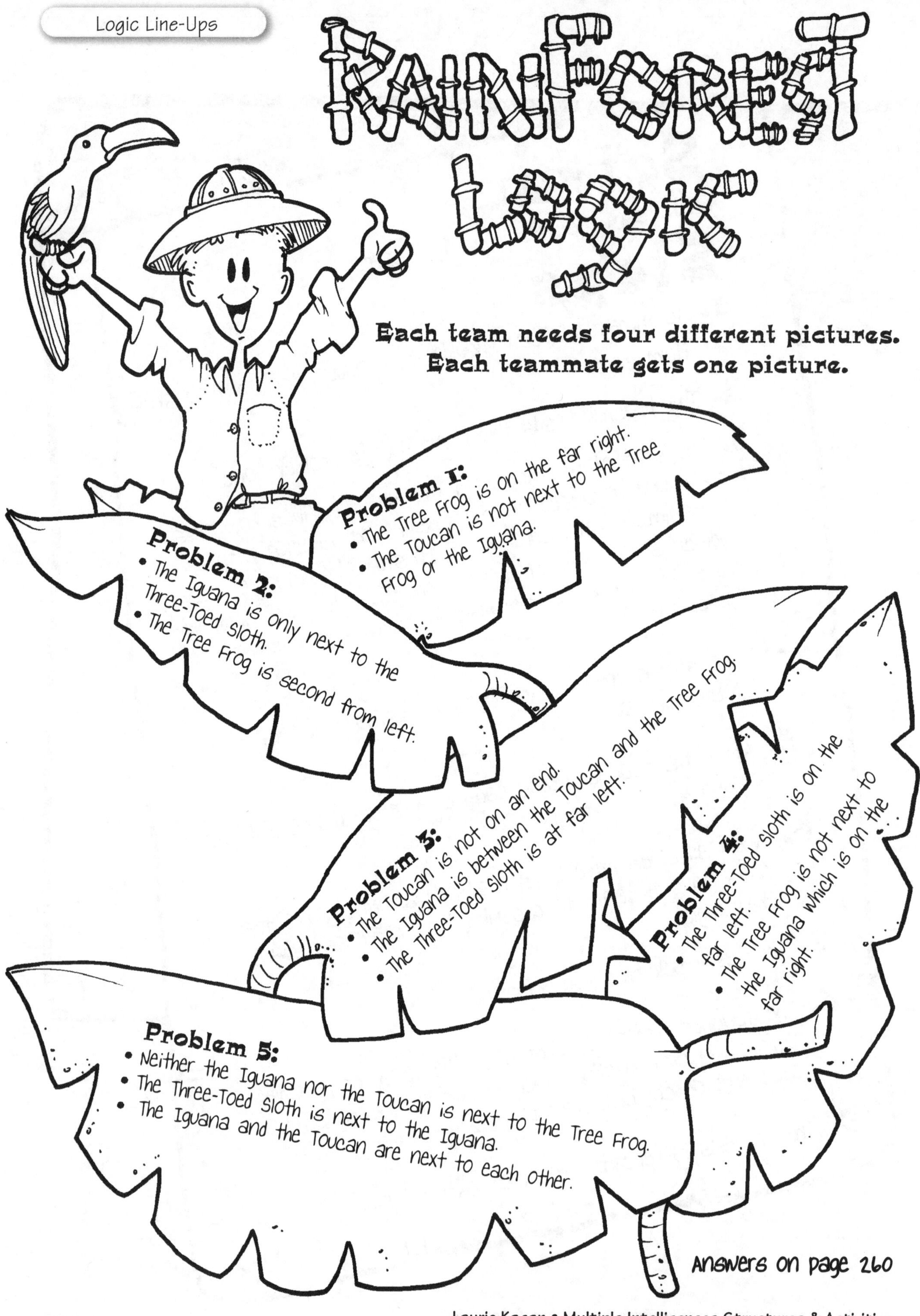
Rainforest Logic
Each team needs four different pictures.
Each teammate gets one picture.
Problem 1:
• The Tree Frog is on the far right.
• The Toucan is not next to the Tree Frog or the Iguana.
Problem 2:
• The Iguana is only next to the Three-Toed sloth.
• The Tree Frog is second from left.
Problem 3:
• The Toucan is not on an end.
• The Iguana is between the Toucan and the Tree Frog.
• The Three-Toed sloth is at far left.
Problem 4:
• The Three-Toed sloth is on the far left.
• The Tree Frog is not next to the Iguana which is on the far right.
Problem 5:
• Neither the Iguana nor the Toucan is next to the Tree Frog.
• The Three-Toed sloth is next to the Iguana.
• The Iguana and the Toucan are next to each other.
Answers on page 260

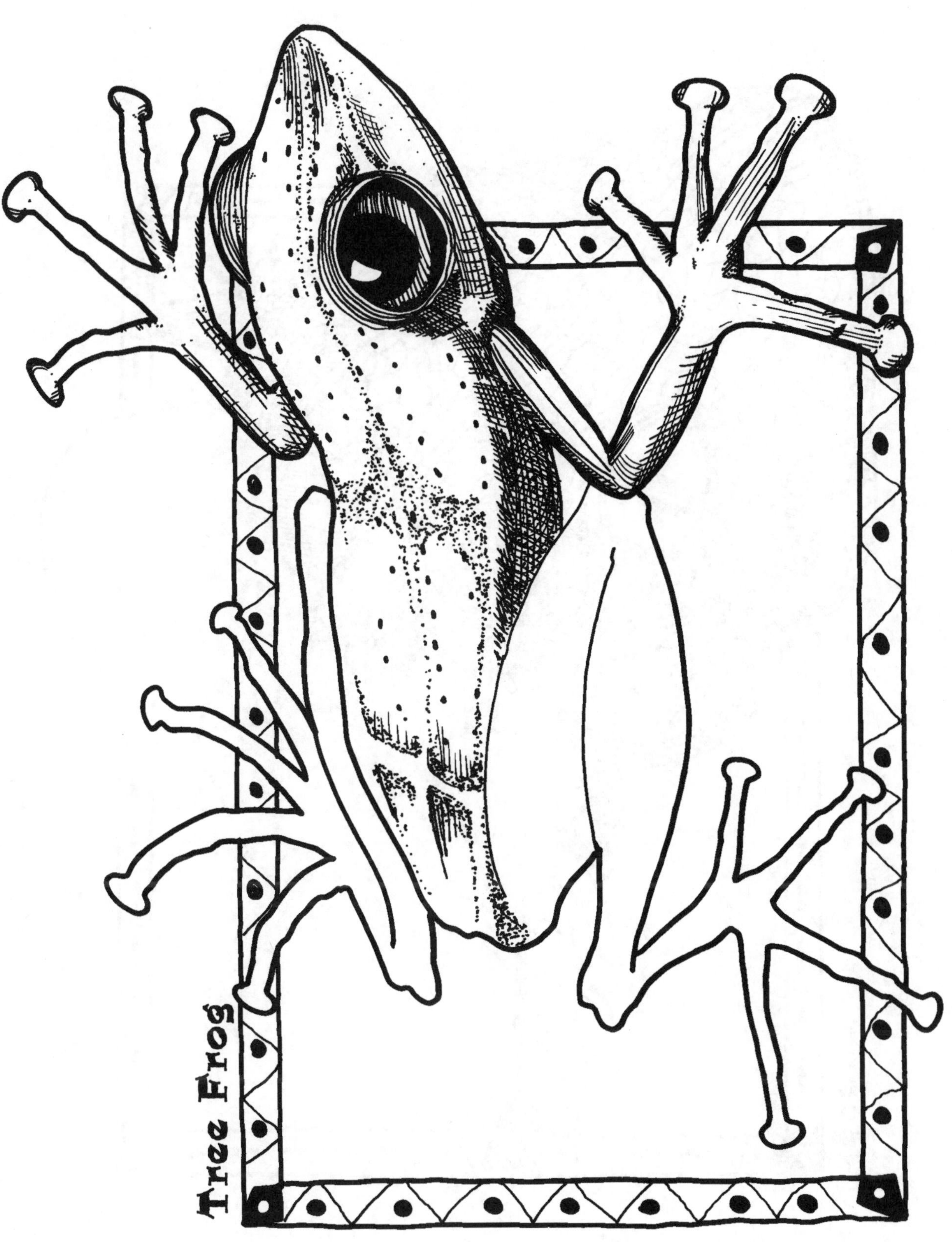
Tree Frog

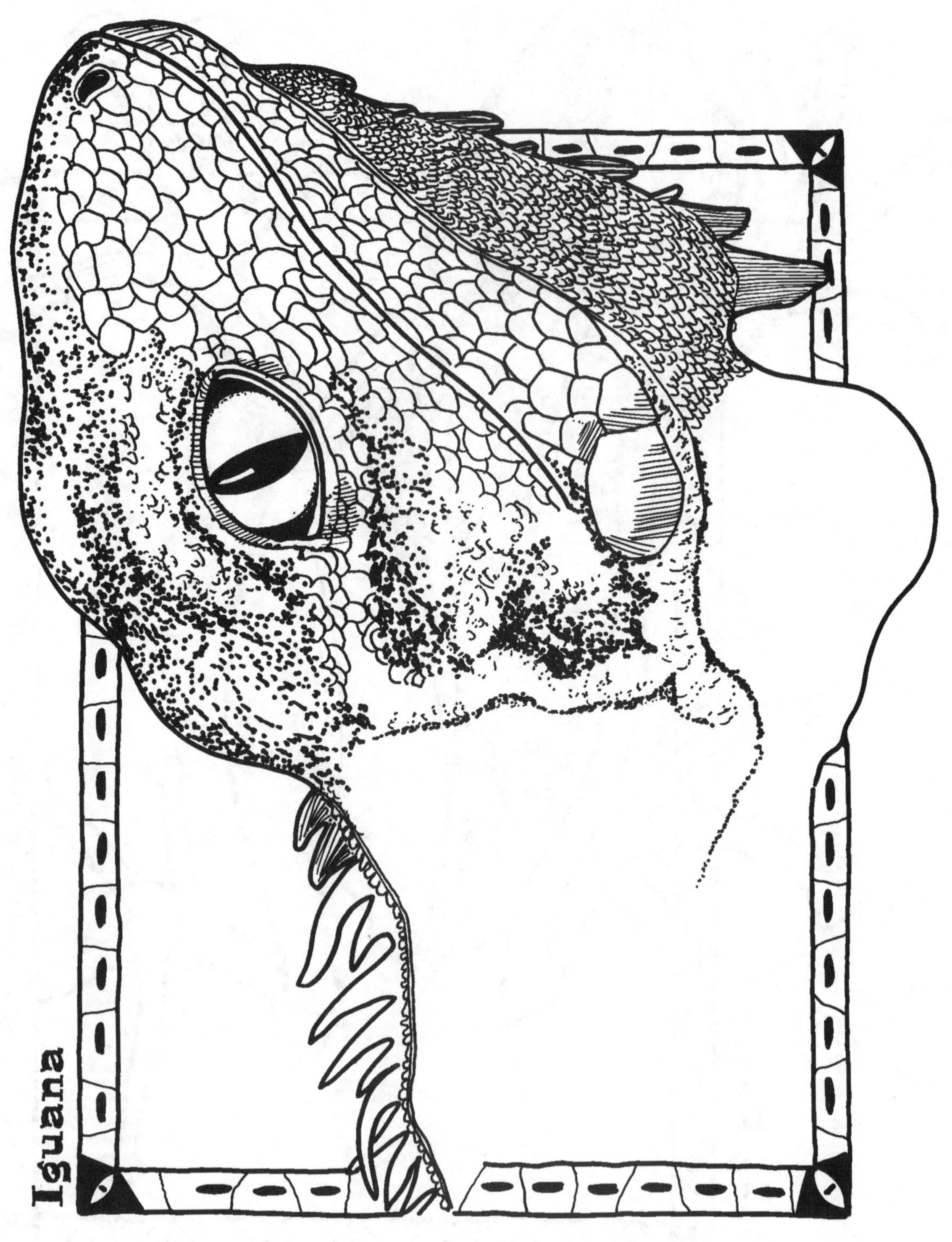
Iguana

Three-Toed Sloth

Toucan

Each person on the team needs one student card.

Problem 1:
Line up by the number of letters in teammember's first name, least amount to greatest amount.

Problem 2:
- The four students are lined up by age, youngest to oldest.
- Patrick is not the youngest and was born after Joe.
- Joe is not the oldest.
- Maria was born after Patrick.

Problem 3:
- The four students are lined up by height, shortest to tallest.
- Toby wishes he was tallest, but isn't.
- Maria is 2" taller than Patrick and 5" shorter than Joe.
- Patrick is shorter than Toby by 3".

Problem 4:
- Neither Patrick nor Joe were next to Toby.
- Maria was next to Joe.

Problem 5:
- Joe and Toby are standing next to each other.
- Patrick is not first or last.
- There is one person between Toby and Maria.

Answers on page 261

Toby

Patrick

Maria

Joe

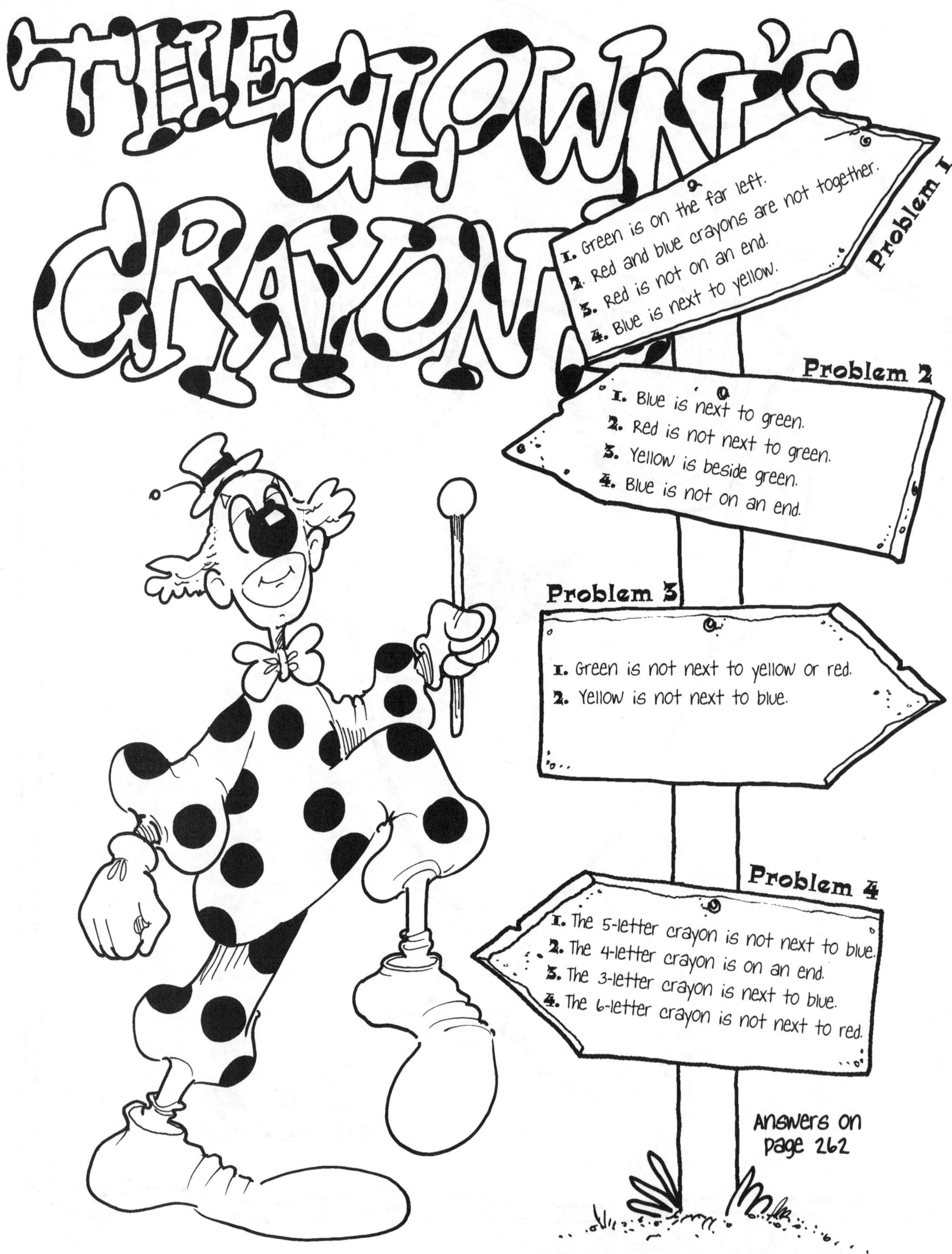
THE CLOWN'S CRAYONS
Problem 1
1. Green is on the far left.
2. Red and blue crayons are not together.
3. Red is not on an end.
4. Blue is next to yellow.
Problem 2
1. Blue is next to green.
2. Red is not next to green.
3. Yellow is beside green.
4. Blue is not on an end.
Problem 3
1. Green is not next to yellow or red.
2. Yellow is not next to blue.
Problem 4
1. The 5-letter crayon is not next to blue.
2. The 4-letter crayon is on an end.
3. The 3-letter crayon is next to blue.
4. The 6-letter crayon is not next to red.
Answers on page 262

Yellow

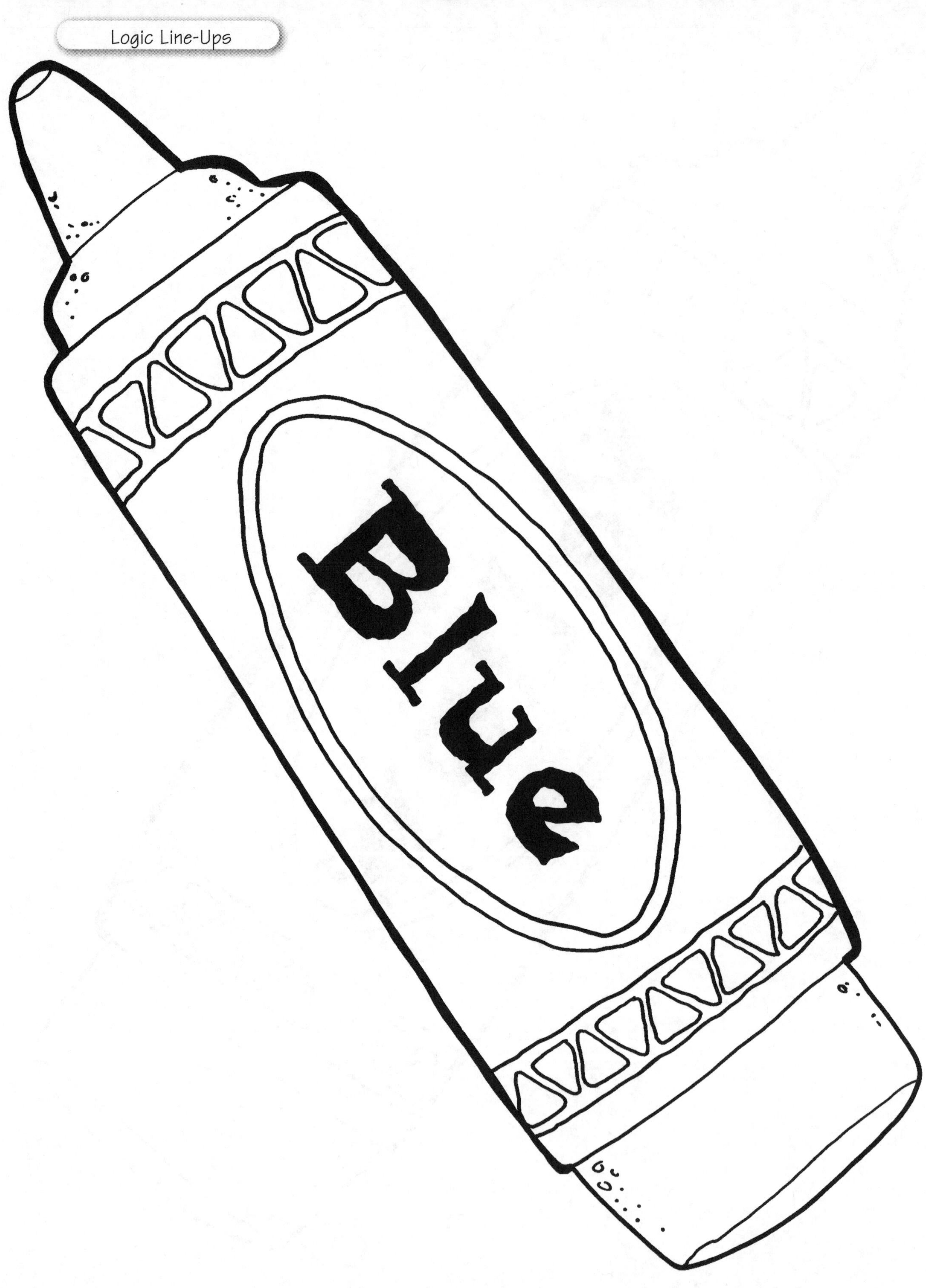
Blue

Green

Red

Pocket Change
Clue cards
Problem 1
1. First comes twenty pennies plus a nickel.
2. Last is eight pennies minus three pennies.
3. Thirteen take away 12 is second.
Problem 2
1. One dime take away a nickel is not on an end.
2. Twenty-six pennies minus a quarter is next to the nickel.
3. The value of two nickels is first.
4. Two dimes and a nickel is next to ten cents.
Problem 3
1. The value of five pennies plus a nickel is not on an end.
2. A quarter minus two dimes is next to the penny.
3. The dime is next to the value of five nickels.
Problem 4
1. The value of one dime, two nickels, and five pennies is not next to the dime or penny.
2. One cent comes first.
Answers on page 262

Nickel

Dime

Penny

Quarter

Mom, Dad, Sister, and Brother are in the car; two are in the front seat and two are in the back.

Students stand up holding their picture cards to solve this 2 x 2 puzzle.

Problem 1

1. Dad is not driving.
2. The son is not behind dad.
3. Mom is in the front seat.
4. Dad is not in a back seat.

Problem 2

1. Dad is taking his family for a drive.
2. Mom is not next to her daughter.
3. The sister is behind her dad.

Answers on page 263

Problem 3

1. The sister and brother are not next to each other.
2. Dad turns around to talk to Mom.
3. The daughter is kitty-corner to her dad, who is not driving.

Problem 4

1. The sister is not old enough to drive.
2. The brother is in front of Mom.
3. The sister is not next to her brother or dad.
4. Dad is not driving.

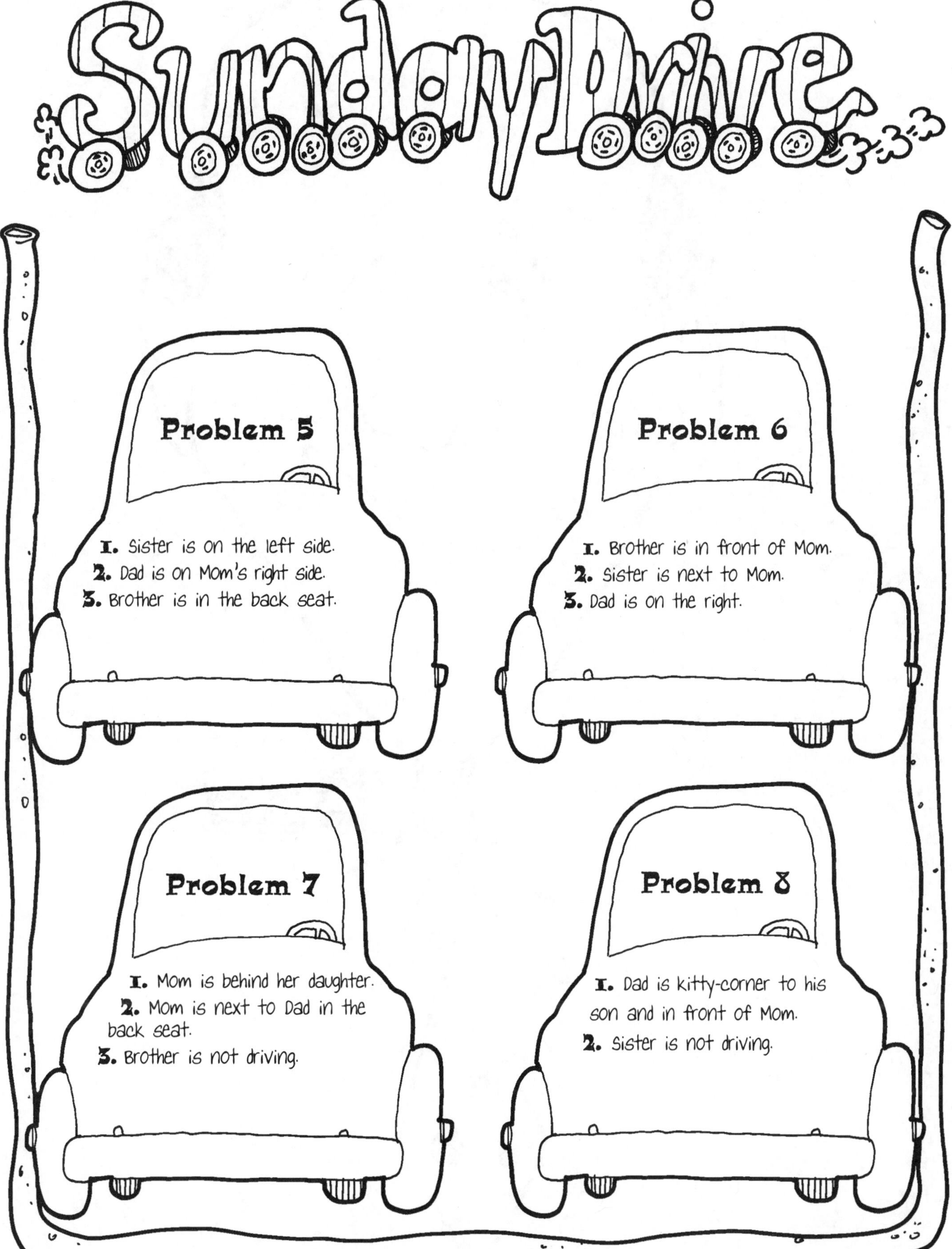
Sunday Drive
Problem 5
1. Sister is on the left side.
2. Dad is on Mom's right side.
3. Brother is in the back seat.
Problem 6
1. Brother is in front of Mom.
2. Sister is next to Mom.
3. Dad is on the right.
Problem 7
1. Mom is behind her daughter.
2. Mom is next to Dad in the back seat.
3. Brother is not driving.
Problem 8
1. Dad is kitty-corner to his son and in front of Mom.
2. Sister is not driving.

Dad

Mom

Brother

Sister

Students create and sing content songs to familiar tunes.

Multiple Intelligences

- ★ Verbal/Linguistic
- ★★★ Logical/Mathematical
- Visual/Spatial
- ★★★ Musical/Rhythmic
- Bodily/Kinesthetic
- Naturalist
- ★ Interpersonal
- Intrapersonal

Set-up
Teacher may play popular tunes for students to use.
Steps
1. Teacher assigns topics.
2. Students brainstorm words and phrases relating to a topic.
3. Students or teacher select a familiar tune.
4. Students sing original song several times.
5. Students use words and phrases to create new lyrics to the tune.
6. Students share with a partner, team, or the class.

It's Time

Make up a song to wake you up. Choose a familiar tune and rewrite the lyrics.

Title: ______________________________

Tune: ______________________________

What Makes You Angry?

First, list the things that make you angry. Then select a familiar tune and write a song about being angry.

Title: ______________________________

Tune: ______________________________

School is Cool

Make up a song about school using the tune to "Three Blind Mice."

Title: ______________________________

Samuel Clemens

Tune: Frère Jacques

Samuel Clemens, Samuel Clemens
Did you know, he's Mark Twain?
Born 1835
When Halley's comet arrived
Did you know, he's Mark Twain?

Worked at a newspaper,
Was a river pilot
Mark Twain wrote Tom Sawyer
Wrote Huckleberry Finn
Died April 1910
That's Mark Twain, that's Mark Twain.

Laura Ingalls

Tune: B-I-N-G-O

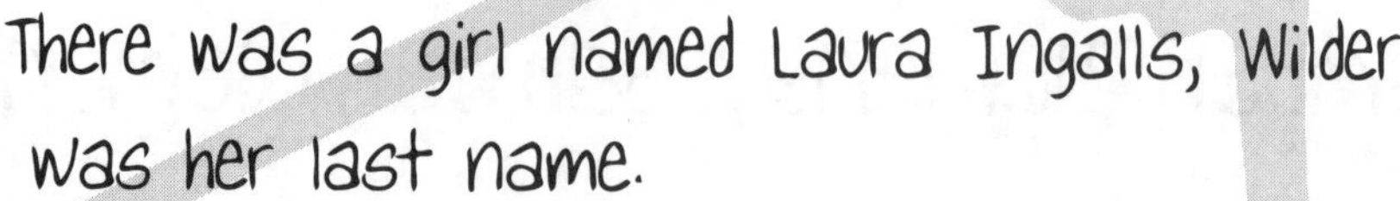

There was a girl named Laura Ingalls, Wilder was her last name.

Chorus: L-A-U-R-A, L-A-U-R-A, L-A-U-R-A, Laura Ingalls Wilder.

The little girl name Laura, was born in Pepin, Wisconsin.

Chorus

She moved to Walnut Grove, and met and married Alonzo.

Chorus

One year later Rose was born, she joined the traveling family.

Chorus

They moved around and finally found a farm in Rocky Ridge.

Chorus

On this farm the biggest crops were books and books that Laura wrote.

Chorus

It's sad to say it came to an end when Laura would never write again.

Chorus

She lived a life of 90 years and wrote 11 stories.

Chorus

AEIOU

Make up a song about the vowels using the tune to "Row, Row, Row Your Boat."

Title: ____

3's Table

Tune: Jingle Bells

Three, six, nine,
Twelve, fifteen,
Eighteen, twenty-one...
Twenty-four,
Twenty-seven,
Thirty, thirty-three,
Ohhh!
Three, six, nine,
Twelve, fifteen,
Eighteen, twenty-one...
Twenty-four,
Twenty-seven,
Thirty, thirty-three!

The Gallon Man

Tune: Ants Go Marching

Two pints go marching two by two, Hurrah! Hurrah!
Two pints go marching two by two, Hurrah! Hurrah!

As doubles they plunge into a quart, standing so
quiet, as if they're in court....As they all go marching
into the chest to get out of the rain.

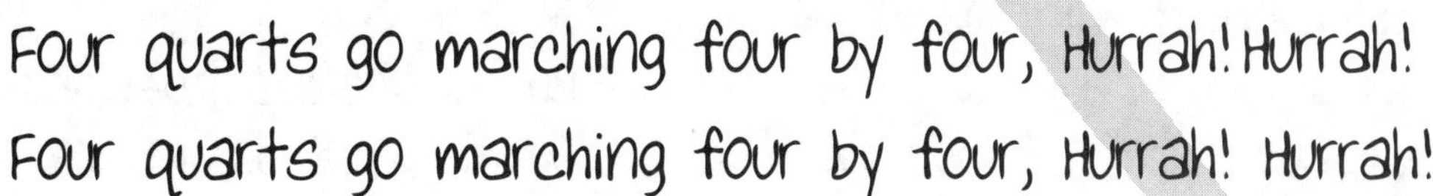

Four quarts go marching four by four, Hurrah! Hurrah!
Four quarts go marching four by four, Hurrah! Hurrah!

All four follow and slip inside, standing so close
as if they were tied...As they all go marching into
the chest to get out of the rain.

A gallon goes marching one by one, Hurrah! Hurrah!
A gallon goes marching one by one, Hurrah! Hurrah!

Add together eight pints or four quarts,
the total is always one gallon of course!
As they all go marching-equivalent-and-dry-
out of the rain.

When The Signs Come Marching In

Tune: When the Saints Come Marching In

Verse 1
Oh When the signs, come marching in,
Oh When the signs come marching in,
We will learn how to **add** them,
When the signs come marching in...

Verse 2
Oh yes we know, Oh yes we know,
When the signs are both the same,
We will **add** both the numbers,
And the sign, it will remain!

Verse 3
But when they're not, but when they're not,
The equation begins anew,
Subtract the negative from the positive
And your problems will be through...

Verse 4
Oh when the signs come marching in!
Oh when the signs come marching in!
We will learn how to **subtract** them,
When those signs come marching in.

Verse 5
This may sound hard, but it is not,
The thing you must remember to do,
First change the sign of the second number,
And add like you always do.

Verse 6
Oh when those signs come marching in,
Oh when those signs come marching in,
We will learn how to **times** them,
When the signs come marching in.

Verse 7
To multiply, to multiply,
If the signs are both the same,
We just **times** both the numbers,
But the positive sign will remain.

Verse 8
But if one's a plus, and the other's not,
Oh my what do we do? We **times** both the numbers,
But negative will be the new!

Verse 9
And to divide, and to divide,
We know just what to do,
We use the rules to multiply,
But instead we **divide** the two.

Verse 10
Oh when those signs come marching in,
Oh when those signs come marching in,
We all know what to do,
when the signs come marching in!

by Lisa Pazinko, New Jersey

Name ______________________________ Date ____________________

A. First sing the first two verses of "When the Signs Come Marching In"

(Addition: same signs)

1. $-6 + (-4) =$
2. $\begin{array}{r} -6 \\ \underline{-2} \end{array}$
3. $6 + 9 =$
4. $\begin{array}{r} 7 \\ \underline{+14} \end{array}$
5. $12 + 3 + 4 =$
6. $\begin{array}{r} -6 \\ \underline{-3} \end{array}$
7. $-7 + (-2) =$

B. Now sing the third verse!

(Addition: different signs)

1. $14 + (-3) =$
2. $\begin{array}{r} -6 \\ \underline{+5} \end{array}$
3. $16 + (-2) =$
4. 3 plus -9
5. $15 + (-9) =$
6. $14 + (-7) =$

C. Now sing the fourth and fifth verse!

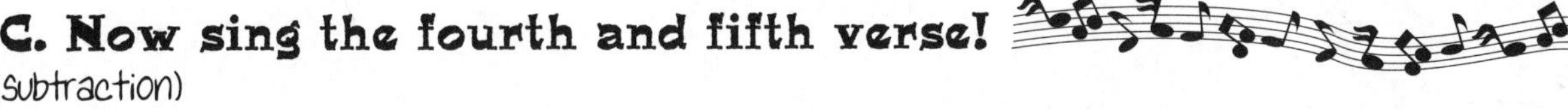

(subtraction)

1. $15 - (-4) =$
2. $14 - (-3) =$
3. $7 - (-7) =$
4. $-15 - 7 =$
5. $10 - (-6) =$

continued next page

Name ______________________________ Date ____________________

D. Sing the sixth and seventh verses!

(Multiplication: same signs)

1. (-6) (-4) = 2. 7(3) = 3. (-2) (-3) =

E. Sing verse eight!

(Multiplication: different signs)

1. (-6) (4) = 2. -3 (7) = 3. (-8) (2) =

4. (-2) (6) =

F. Sing the ninth and tenth verses!

(Division)

1. 14 ÷ -2 = 2. 15 ÷ -5= 3. -15 divided by 5 =

4. $-7\overline{)21}$ 5. 25 divided by -5 = 6. -25 ÷ 5 =

7. 8 ÷ -4 =

Math Music

Make up a song about math.
Remember to select a simple tune.

Title: ______________________________

Tune: ______________________________

Louis Pasteur

Tune: Twinkle, Twinkle Little Star

Louie, Louie, you're our star.
You saved lives and took us far.
Anthrax, rabies, milk, and more,
Gave your life to open doors.
Louie, Louie, you're our star.
Thanks so much! You took us far.

Jacques Cousteau

Tune: Gilligan's Island

Sit right back and I'll tell you a tale, A tale of Jacques Cousteau...A Frenchman who loved his machines, film, and the water below.

As a boy he caused some trouble, breaking many rules.
His parents were unhappy with him...sending him to boarding school.

As a navy man he sailed around the ocean blue.
He married Simone and had 2 sons; Jean and Pierre were the two.

The Calypso was the ship he sailed, to see the coral reef.
He searched a sunken ship and saw fish beyond belief.

Then he left the Navy and became a TV star.
He filmed his travels with his crew, and shared them with the world.

One day in 1985, a medal he received,
For helping save the oceans blue, And teaching what he believed.

Water Cycle

Tune: Clementine

Evaporation,
condensation,
Precipitation falling down.
These are all parts
of the
water cycle,
It just goes
around and
'round.

The Solar System

List items in the solar system. Then make up a song using the tune to "London Bridge Is Falling Down."

Title: ______________________________

The Seasons

Winter, Spring, Summer, or Fall? Pick a season and write a song about it using the tune "Hickory, Dickory, Dock."

Title: ______________________________

Christopher Columbus

Tune: Itsy Bitsy Spider

Christopher Columbus went sailing
'cross the sea.
Everyone said "sail east!"
But Chris said, "West is for me."
Isabella gave him ships
Three ships fast and true,
So Christopher Columbus could
sail the ocean blue.

In 1492 he set sail with the tide,
A shortcut to the Indies
Was what he hoped to find.
On October 12th,
The ship struck solid ground.
He thought he'd reached the Indies,
But America he found.

Colonial Times

Tune: Yankee Doodle

I like the colonial times,
With all the Founding Fathers,
And all the things they brought with them,
From England, the Great
"Mother."
Homesteading, and building
towns,
Forming a new nation,
Farming, building industry,
Increasing immigration.

Seeking Freedom

Tune: Yankee Doodle

In colonial times there were a lot of changes in our nation
seeking freedom of all kinds, including education,
In colonial times there were a lot of changes in our nation
seeking freedom of all kinds, including education.

They came for religion, they came by choice,
They came for many reasons.
But they were taxed without a voice,
And soon accused of treason.

Rebellion started to erupt with talk of liberty,
In protest they dumped in Boston Harbor lots
of England's tea!

Give me liberty, or give me death,
It was the Age of Reason.
The Revolution had begun,
And Redcoats were in season!

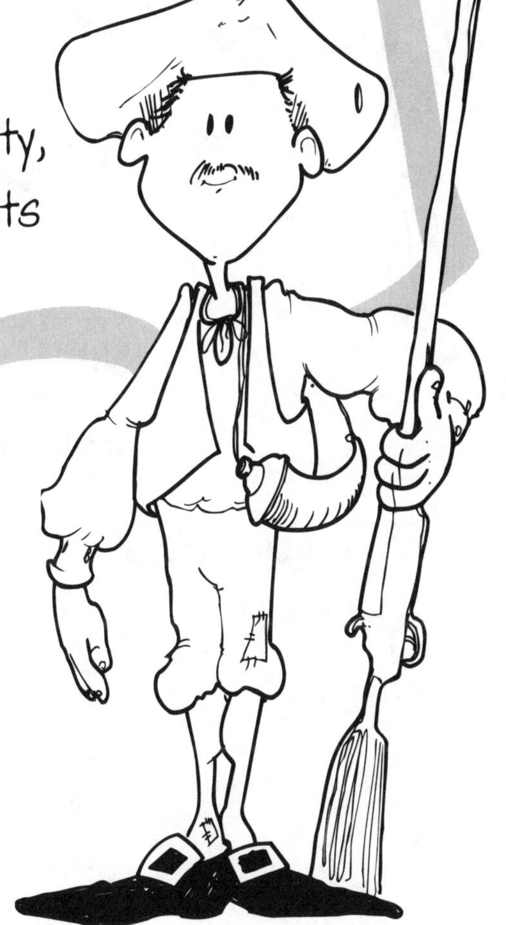

Christopher Columbus

Tune: Row, Row, Row Your Boat

Chris, Chris, Christopher,
Columbus was his name.
Isabella was the Queen
Of the land of Spain.

Sail, sail, sail three ships,
Across the ocean sea.
Gold and spices he would find,
When he reached the Indies.

Nina, Pinta, Santa Maria,
Full of sailors grand.
Fearful, ready to give up,
Until they sighted land.

Ben Franklin

Tune: Twinkle, Twinkle, Little Star

Old Ben said, "A penny saved,"
Store it, it's a penny earned."

"Fish and visitors do not keep,
Three days max, cuz both will
stink."

"Eat to live, not live to
eat." Old Ben's advice, you
can't beat!

Independence!

Tune: Yankee Doodle

Yankee Doodle went to town, he was a minuteman.
He wanted Freedom and his rights, he'd fight to make his stand.

Chorus: Independence was his goal, freedom was his right.
The people here were determined, to take a stand and fight.

The British sent the Redcoats in, taxes were too high,
King George was a real strong-head, Ben Franklin told him why.

Chorus

The revolt was in the air, the British fired upon us,
Washington was there to lead, for Liberty and Justice!

Chorus

The colonists had victory, Great Britain was defeated,
America was born - brand new, the colonies had freedom!

Thomas Jefferson

Tune: Partridge in a Pear Tree

Thomas Jefferson was a president,
He had many talents,
Was a founding father,
Wrote the D. of I.,
Spoke six languages,
He became a lawyer,
Played the violin,
He built Monticello,
Founded a University,
Was a naturalist,
Invented many things,
Had a huge garden,
And loved to eat ice cream!

Pocahontas

Tune: Frère Jacques

Pocahontas, Pocahontas,
Played in the woods, whenever she could.
She met two white-faced strangers, didn't think of dangers,
She was brave, very brave.

She met John Smith, she saved his head,
Or he'd be dead, not in his bed.
Then he went to England, didn't ever see him again,
She was sad, very sad.

Then came John Rolfe, they got married.
Off they went, to another continent.
She made such a fine wife, and they lived a good life
She was happy, very happy.

Pocahontas, Pocahontas, something bad,
something sad,
It was cold and drafty, she wasn't
feeling snappy,
soon she died, history hasn't lied.

Gold Rush

Tune: She'll Be Comin' 'round the Mountain

We'll be riding on that stagecoach when we come
We'll be riding on that stagecoach when we come
We'll be riding on that stagecoach, We'll be riding on that stagecoach
We'll be riding on that stagecoach when we come

We'll be riding for freedom when we come
We'll be riding for freedom when we come
We'll be riding for freedom, if you join us you will get some
We'll be riding for freedom when we come

Because now we got a break to stake our claim
Because now we got a break to stake our claim
Because now we got a break, Because now we got a break
Because now we got a break to stake our claim.

Going to settle California when we come
Going to settle California when we come
Going to settle California, Going to settle California,
Going to settle California when we come.

Wild, Wild West

Tune: Winter Wonderland

Gunfire sounds, are you listenin'
People run, bullets hissin'.
The outlaws are here, and there's lots of fear
Living in the wild, wild west.

On the plains, cattle roamin'
Wagon trains, ruts are growin'
The people are tough, the land's free and rough,
Taming the wild, wild west.

On the prairie you can build a campfire,
Boiling coffee and baking beans,
Cowboys standing quietly on the hillside,
Dream of girls they've never even seen.

Stories told, are you listenin'
Rumors of streams where gold is glistenin'
Fortunes are made and merchants are paid
Building the wild, wild west.

Pony Express

Tune: I've Been Working on the Railroad

I've been riding on my pony,
Across the wide prairie...
I've been trying to deliver the mail,
Through all this misery.

Through rain, and sleet, and stormy weather-
And Indian arrows too.
I change my horse at every station,
For the mail must go through.

Chorus:
Pony won't you go, pony won't you go
Through the night and morn'
Pony won't you go, pony won't you go
Into the tales of yore

When I reach my destination,
I jump down from my horse
I hand the mail to the next rider,
And head for the saloon...of course!

The air is thick and smoky,
With sweaty gamblers galore!
I gulped root beer quite quickly,
And hit the trail once more.

Chorus

Abraham Lincoln

Tune: She'll Be Comin' 'round the Mountain

Abraham Lincoln was our 16th president,
Abraham Lincoln was our 16th president,
When the civil war was storming,
And our country was in mourning,
Abe Lincoln gave the Gettysburg address.

Abe Lincoln freed the slaves and
won the war,
Abe Lincoln freed the slaves
and won the war,
All men are created equal,
But with Abe there's no sequel,
Abe Lincoln was our greatest
president.

From Our View

Tune: Amazing Grace

Oh Mother Earth,
and Father sky,
Your precious children weep.
Our land destroyed,
Our people lost,
We feel our spirit die.

From o'er the plains
The white man came,
With blinded eyes and greed.
Their gods and guns,
Disease and ways,
Left us forever changed.

Flapper

Tune: When the Saints Come Marching In

Oh in the 20's, the roaring 20's,
Party time for everyone.
Along came the flapper dresses
And the mighty Charleston.

Oh kicking feet, and crossing knees,
And swinging beads, and having fun.
Alas, for me I was no dancer,
So a wall flower I'd become.

Celebrate History

Go back in time and list items and events. Then write a song about that period of time to the tune of "I'm a Little Teapot."

Title: ____

Students discover attributes that are the same and different in two pictures or objects.

Multiple Intelligences

- ★★★ Verbal/Linguistic
- ★★★ Logical/Mathematical
- ★★★ Visual/Spatial
- Musical/Rhythmic
- Bodily/Kinesthetic
- ★★★ Naturalist
- ★★★ Interpersonal
- Intrapersonal

Set-up

Two pictures or ojects (many ways the same, many ways different), one answer sheet, and one barrier (or paperclipped laminated pictures).

Steps

1. Students, in pairs or teams, interact, each describing their own picture or object. Many forms of interaction are possible including:
   - Talking
   - Writing
   - Writing essays about the pictures
   - Drawing pictures to pass to each other
   - Acting out the pictures
   - Discussing the pictures from memory with pictures out of sight.
2. Students take turns recording similarities and differences.

Recording Sheet
Same
Different

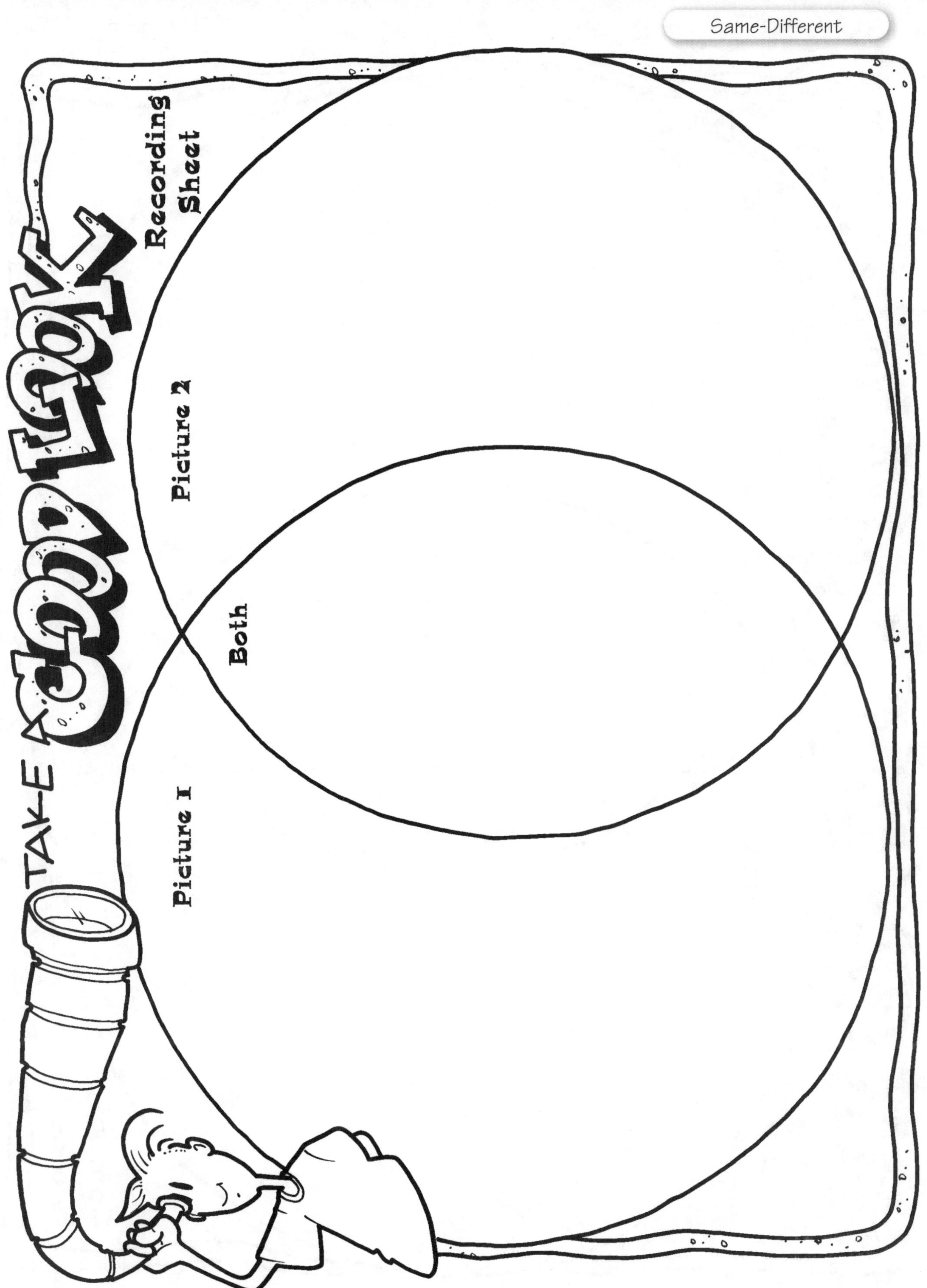
TAKE A GOOD LOOK
Recording Sheet
Picture 1
Both
Picture 2

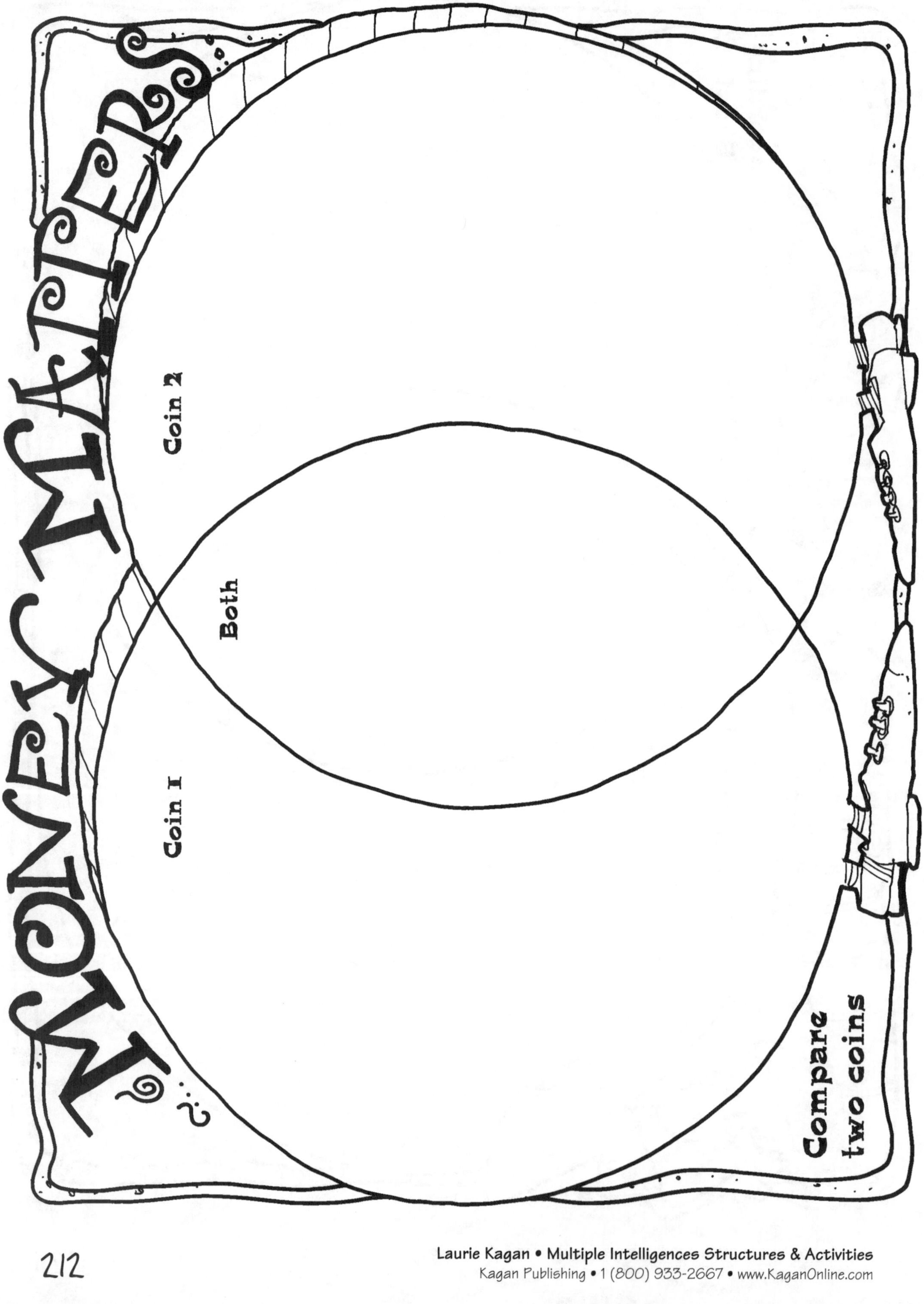

MONEY MATTERS

Coin 1

Both

Coin 2

Compare two coins

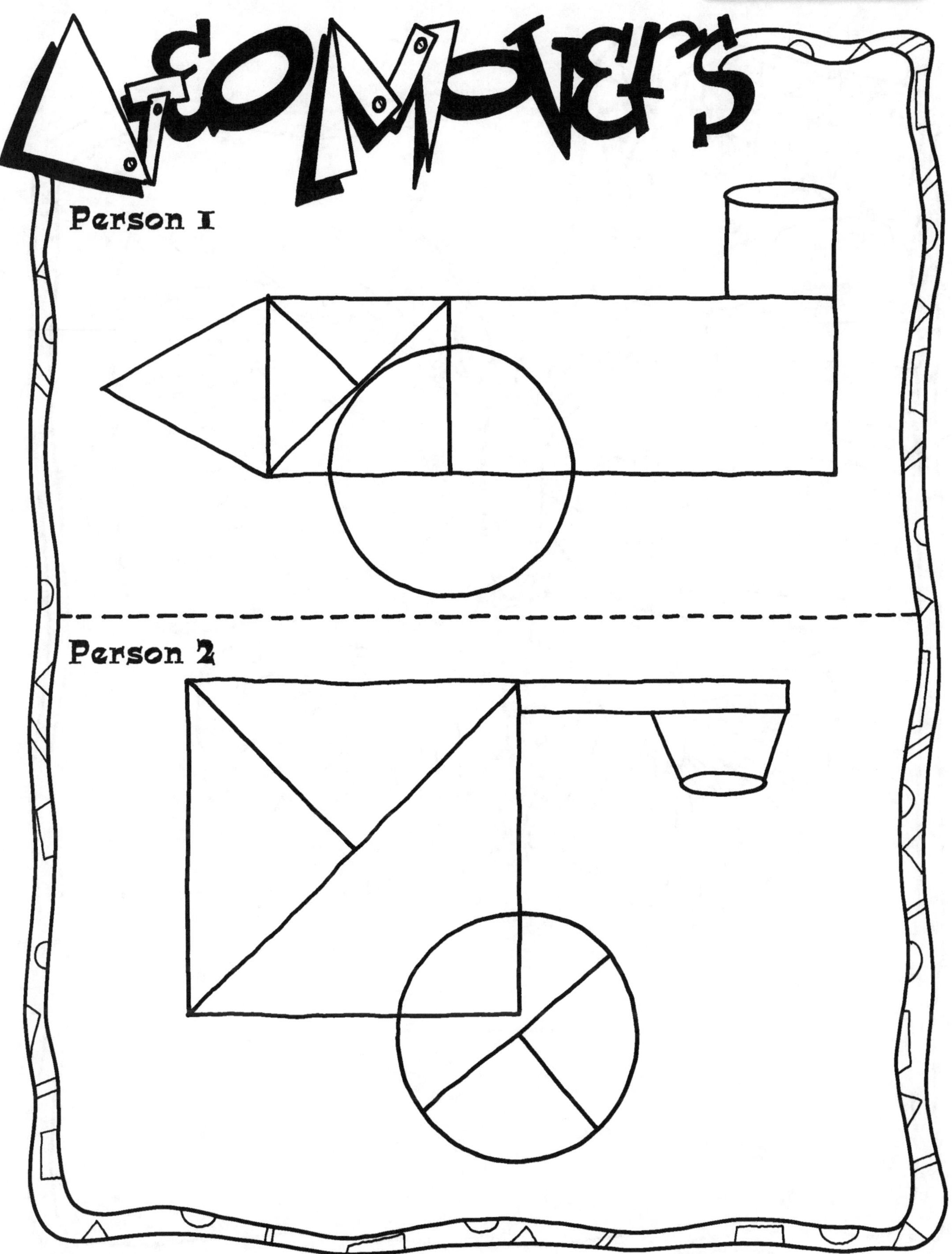
GeoMovers
Person 1
Person 2

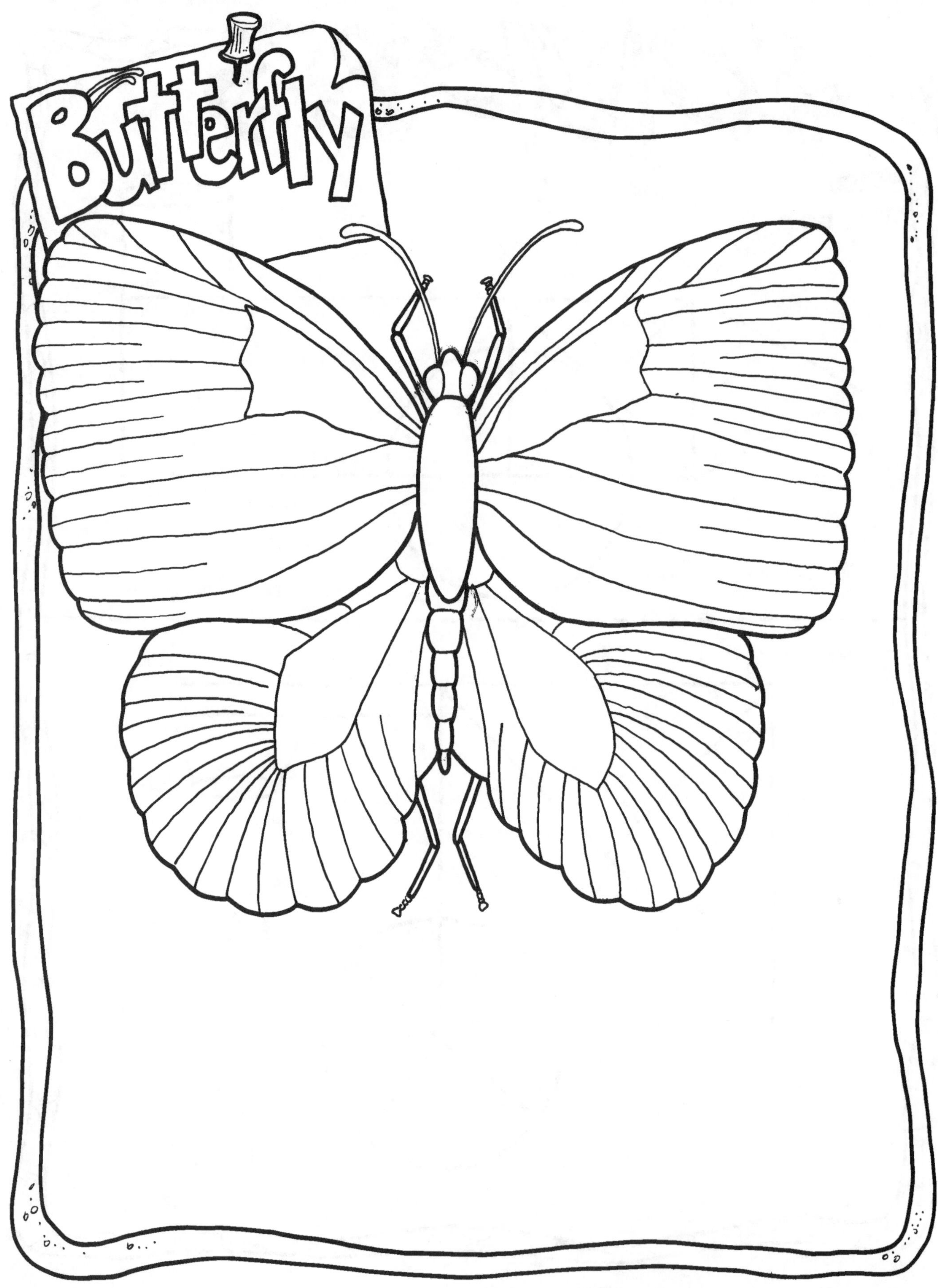
Butterfly

Moth

People sometimes mistake me for a moth; perhaps it's because I have four broad thin wings and beautiful colors. I also have two antennae on my head that look like tiny horns with knobs on the end.

As you watch me fly, you'll see my four beautiful wings move separately. At rest, I close my wings vertically over my back - almost like pages of a book. Both sides of my wings are covered with very tiny scales that fit closely together like the scales of a fish. Be careful not to touch my wings, because your fingers will rub off my scales. Each scale is so small it seems like it's brightly colored dust.

It's my scales that make my beautiful markings. Each scale is all one color, and patches of the same colored scales give me my patterns. It's easy to appreciate my colors because I generally fly during the day.

Getting my wings took me many stages. First, I went through the egg stage. Second came the caterpillar, or larva stage. In this stage, I loved to go into gardens and eat the leaves off a vegetable plant or tree. The third stage I went through was the pupa, or chrysalis stage. When I was in this stage, my skin became very hard and dry - I looked dead. My pupa also looked angular with my sides flattened and my corners or edges sharp.

I come in many colors and sizes. My size varies from less than the diameter of a dime to six or seven inches across with my wings outstretched. My life span can be quite short - many of us live only a few days. Some live three to five years.

We migrate like birds; we fly north in the spring and south in the fall. Sometimes we fly thousands of miles each way. My friend, the Monarch butterfly, doesn't migrate, but instead finds shelter from the cold and goes to sleep for the winter, hibernating like a bear. The warm sun of spring awakens him and he flitters around the field for weeks before others that had migrated can return.

You know I'm a moth. One of the best indicators is when you see me resting - I'm most comfortable holding my wings out flat from my side, or folding them down against my body.

If you can't find me during the day, it's because I'm hiding in the grass and weeds until twilight. I prefer being out and about in the evenings and night.

I have little hooks or spines that hold the edge of my back wing firmly to my front wing where they overlap. Because they are fastened together, the two broad, thin wings on each side move together.

Some of us have very beautiful colors and markings and people mistake us for butterflies. Our sizes vary. Some of us are so small we could fit on a dime, while others grow to be half a foot. In general, our life span is very short. I also have two antennae on my head which look like long, slender feathers and always taper to a fine point at the end.

I passed through three stages before I got my wings. There was first the egg stage; second the caterpillar, or larva stage; and last the pupa, or chrysalis stage. I barely lived through the caterpillar stage because I'm a pest and cause a great deal of damage.

I love to eat the leaves of garden vegetables and trees. In the pupa stage, my dry, hard caterpillar skin makes me appear to be no longer living. My pupa is smoothly curved and round; I also protect it by spinning a cocoon around it.

When I finally got my wings, they were covered on both sides with very petite fish-like scales that fit closely together. Each scale contains one color, but when they are clustered together it appears that I have spots or patches on my wings. Take care not to touch my wings, because my dust-like scales come off very easily.

There are 20 differences between Fish Bowl #1 and #2. Can you find them?

There are 20 differences between Fish Bowl #1 and #2. Can you find them?

There are 20 differences between Our Town #1 and #2. Can you find them?

There are 20 differences between Our Town #1 and #2. Can you find them?

There are 20 differences between Dino Days #1 and #2. Can you find them?

There are 20 differences between Dino Days #1 and #2. Can you find them?

There are 20 differences between Capt. Coop #1 and #2. Can you find them?

There are 20 differences between Capt. Coop #1 and #2. Can you find them?

#2

There are 20 differences between Welcome Home #1 and #2. Can you find them?

There are 20 differences between Welcome Home #1 and #2. Can you find them?

There are 7 differences between The Train #1 and #2. Can you find them?

There are 7 differences between The Train #1 and #2. Can you find them?

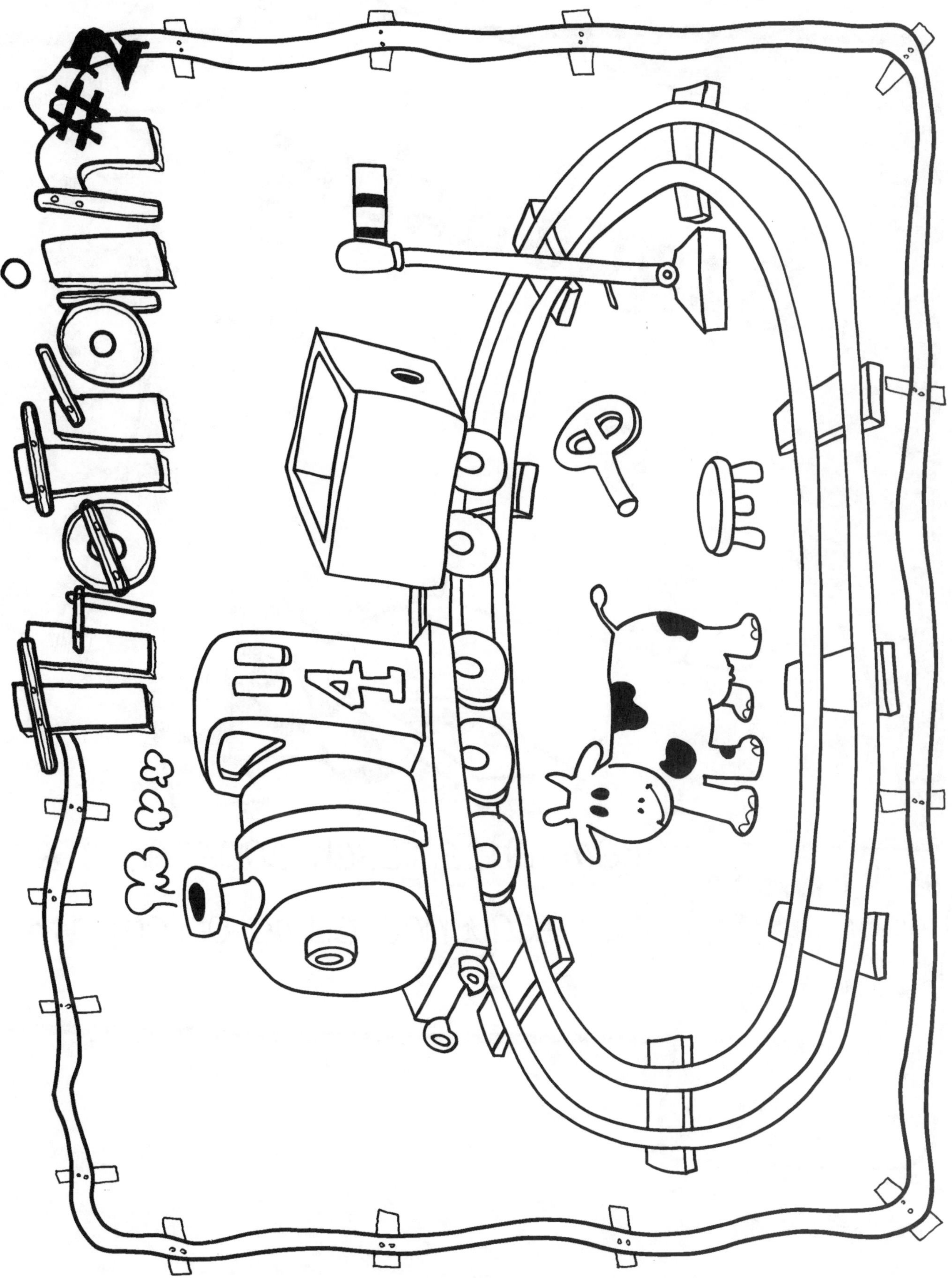

Teammates reach consensus as they sequence cards or objects.

Multiple Intelligences

- ★★ Verbal/Linguistic
- ★★★ Logical/Mathematical
- ★★ Visual/Spatial
- Musical/Rhythmic
- ★ Bodily/Kinesthetic
- ★ Naturalist
- ★★ Interpersonal
- Intrapersonal

Set-up

Teacher prepares objects or cards for students to sequence.

Steps

1. Cards are dealt out, at least one per student.
2. Student one turns one of his/her cards face-up and places it in sequence.
3. All students discuss. If adjustments are made, only student one may move the card.
4. Repeat steps two and three for each student in turn, until all cards are placed.
5. Students check sequence for correctness and celebrate.

Human Happenings

How would your team sequence the great moments in early human history?

cut out cards

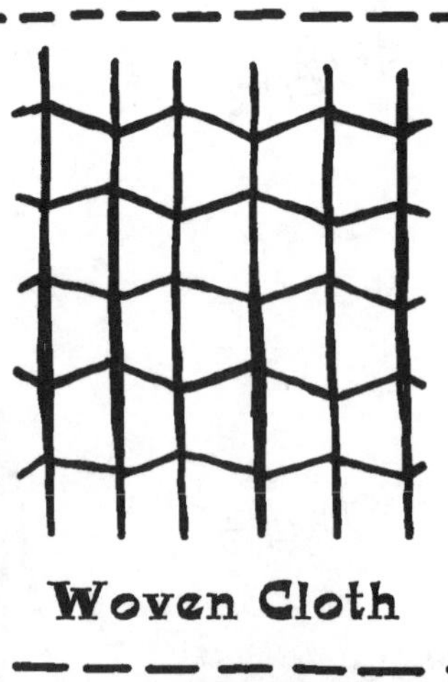

Woven Cloth

Writing

Metal Farming Tools

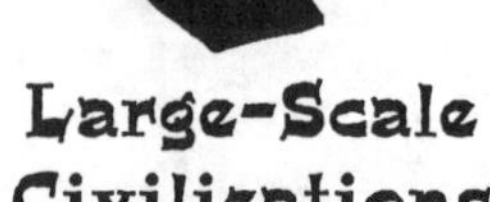

Large-Scale Civilizations

Bow & Arrow

Cave Paintings

Step 1: Pass out 2 cards per teammember.

Step 2: Each student discusses where their card belongs in the sequence. Teams must reach consensus before the card is put in chronological order.

Wheel

Farming Villages

The Great Candy Bar Heist

Can you help the store owner find the candybar robber?

The last student to leave saw the robber. Who was last to leave? What time did each student leave?

Step 1: Pass out 3 cards per teammate.

Step 2: Start by placing card #1 down. Using your observation and thinking skills, discuss and place the flight movements in order.

Step 3: Remember only you can touch your cards!

cut out cards

Mr. Freeman's class got confused. Can you help them put the Pledge of Allegiance back in order?

Step 1: Pass out 3 cards per teammate. Don't let your teammates see your cards.

Step 2: As a team, place the cards in the correct order.

Remember: Everyone must participate. The team must agree on the order.

cut out cards

The Confused Pledge of Allegiance

one nation

with liberty

to the flag

of the United

and justice for all.

I pledge allegiance

for which it stands

and to the republic

under God,

States of

indivisable

America

3 Wise Owls
Put the picture strips in order to find the 3 Wise Owls
cut out cards

Can you put the planets in order?

Using the data on the planet cards, sequence the planets four times in order of:

1. Distance from sun
2. Diameter
3. Length of 1 day
4. Length of planetary year

cut out cards

Earth	**Pluto**	**Saturn**
Maximum distance from sun: 94.5 million miles	**Maximum distance from sun:** 4.6 billion miles	**Maximum distance from sun:** 938 million miles
Diameter: 7,926 miles	**Diameter:** 1,430 miles	**Diameter:** 74,500 miles
Length of day (Rotation time): 23 hours, 56 minutes	**Length of day (Rotation time):** 6 Earth days, 9 hours	**Length of day (Rotation time):** 10 hours, 14 minutes
Length of year (Orbit time): 365.3 Earth Days	**Length of year (Orbit time):** 247.7 Earth years	**Length of year (Orbit time):** 29.5 Earth years

cut out cards

	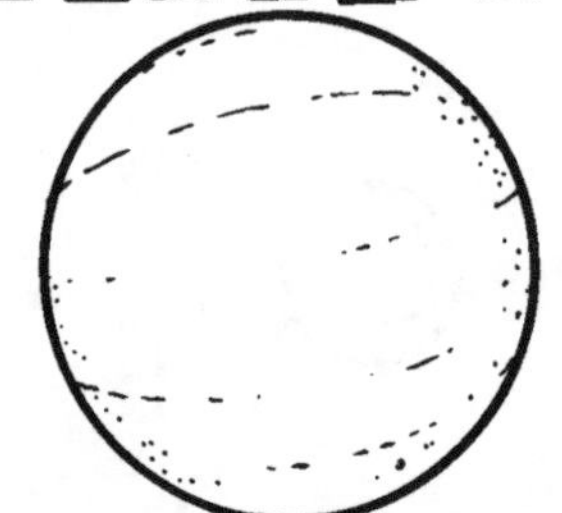	
Venus	**Uranus**	**Mercury**
Maximum distance from sun: 68 million miles	**Maximum distance from sun:** 1.9 billion miles	**Maximum distance from sun:** 43.3 million miles
Diameter: 7,545 miles	**Diameter:** 32,000 miles	**Diameter:** 3,031 miles
Length of day (Rotation time): 117 Earth days	**Length of day (Rotation time):** 17 hours, 14 minutes	**Length of day (Rotation time):** 176 Earth days
Length of year (Orbit time): 224.7 Earth days	**Length of year (Orbit time):** 84 Earth years	**Length of year (Orbit time):** 88 Earth days

cut out cards

Neptune	**Mars**	**Jupiter**
Maximum distance from sun: 2.8 billion miles	**Maximum distance from sun:** 155 million miles	**Maximum distance from sun:** 507 million miles
Diameter: 30,760 miles	**Diameter:** 4,217 miles	**Diameter:** 88,600 miles
Length of day (Rotation time): 17 hours, 6 minutes	**Length of day (Rotation time):** 24 hours, 37.5 minutes	**Length of day (Rotation time):** 9 hours, 50.5 minutes
Length of year (Orbit time): 164.8 Earth years	**Length of year (Orbit time):** 1.8 Earth years	**Length of year (Orbit time):** 11.9 Earth years

Answers worksheet

Maximum distance from sun
closest to furthest

1. ______
2. ______
3. ______
4. ______
5. ______
6. ______
7. ______
8. ______
9. ______

Length of day (Rotation time)
shortest to longest

1. ______
2. ______
3. ______
4. ______
5. ______
6. ______
7. ______
8. ______
9. ______

Diameter
smallest to largest

1. ______
2. ______
3. ______
4. ______
5. ______
6. ______
7. ______
8. ______
9. ______

Length of year (orbit time)
shortest to longest

1. ______
2. ______
3. ______
4. ______
5. ______
6. ______
7. ______
8. ______
9. ______

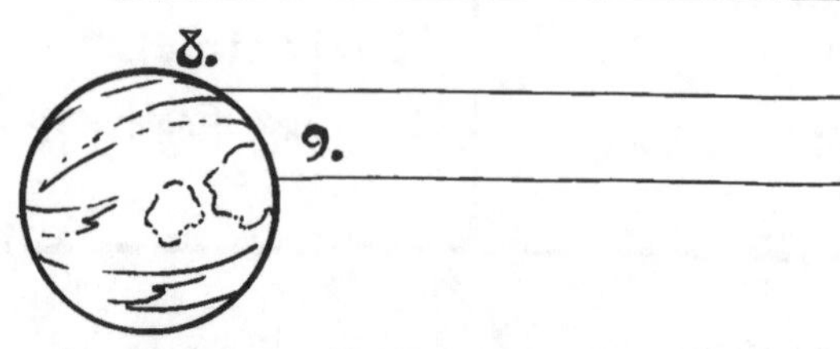

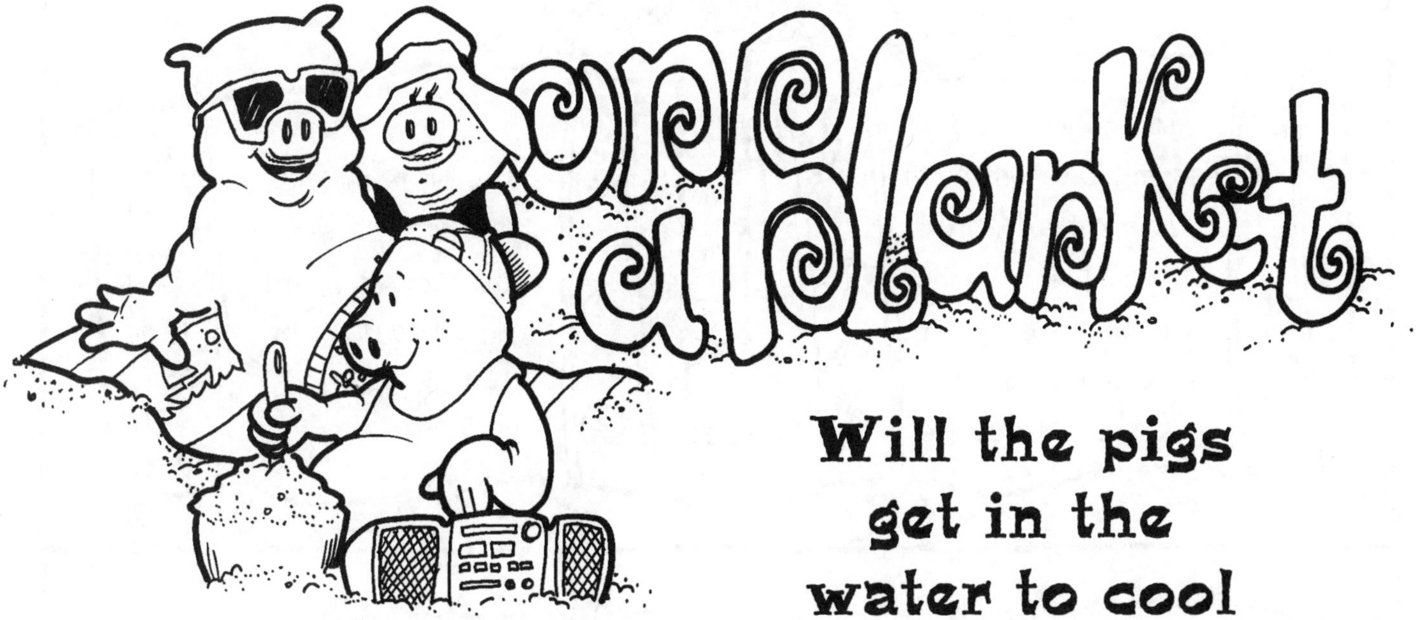

on a Blanket

Will the pigs get in the water to cool off before the beach closes at 5:30?

After reading the story, Pigs on a Blanket, by Amy Axelrod, match the 14 Clue Cards to the corresponding Time Cards.

cut out cards

cut out cards

cut out cards

Time Cards

Match the 14 Time cards with the corresponding Clue cards to solve Pigs on a Blanket!

cut out cards

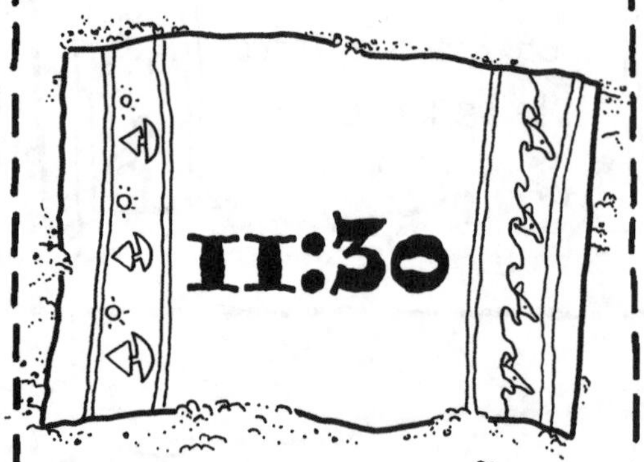

3:02	4:40
12:30	11:30
11:45	3:15

cut out cards
2:55
1:45
12:45
11:40
2:30
5:30
3:30
4:30

Answers

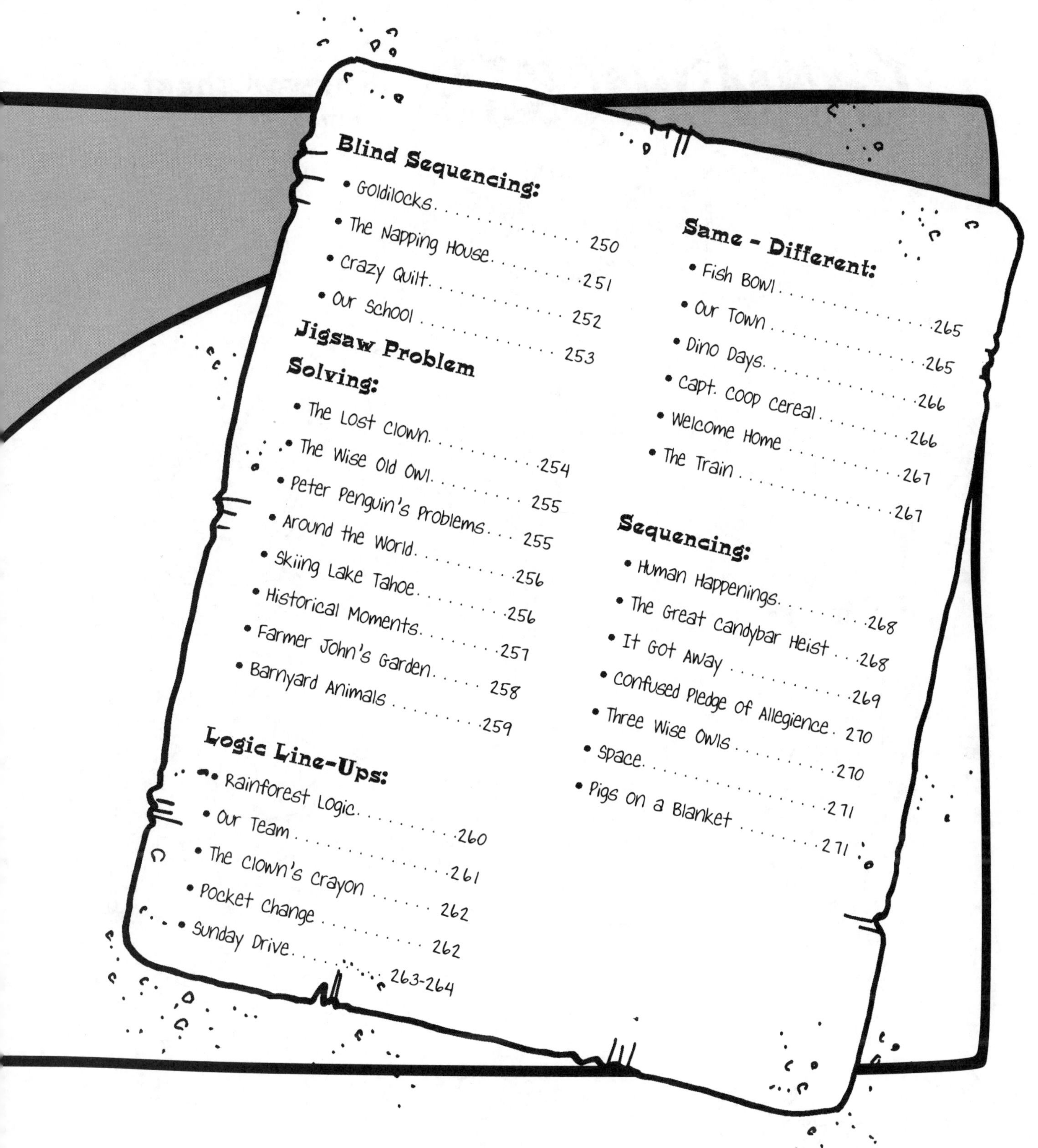

Blind Sequencing:
- Goldilocks 250
- The Napping House 251
- Crazy Quilt 252
- Our School 253

Jigsaw Problem Solving:
- The Lost Clown 254
- The Wise Old Owl 255
- Peter Penguin's Problems . . . 255
- Around the World 256
- Skiing Lake Tahoe 256
- Historical Moments 257
- Farmer John's Garden 258
- Barnyard Animals 259

Logic Line-Ups:
- Rainforest Logic 260
- Our Team 261
- The Clown's Crayon 262
- Pocket Change 262
- Sunday Drive 263-264

Same - Different:
- Fish Bowl 265
- Our Town 265
- Dino Days 266
- Capt. Coop Cereal 266
- Welcome Home 267
- The Train 267

Sequencing:
- Human Happenings 268
- The Great Candybar Heist . . . 268
- It Got Away 269
- Confused Pledge of Allegience . 270
- Three Wise Owls 270
- Space 271
- Pigs on a Blanket 271

Answer sheet

Activity on page 28

Answer sheet

Activity on page 31

1 

2 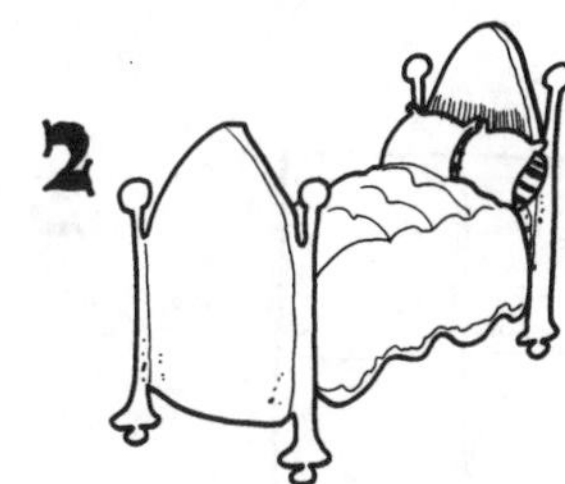

3 

4 

5 

6 

7 

8 

9 

10 

11 

12 

13 

14 

15 

Answer sheet

Activity on page 36

1

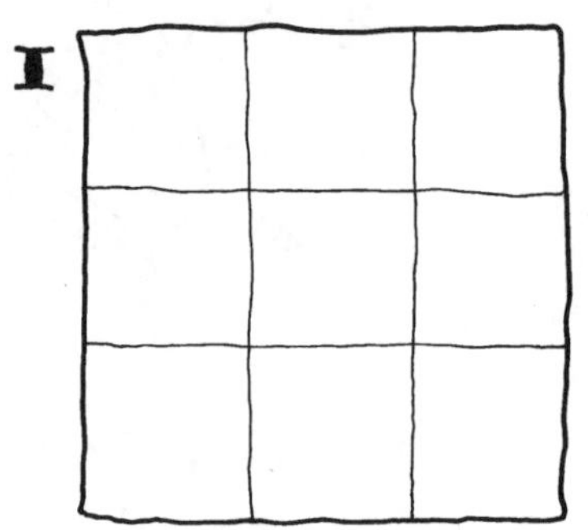

2

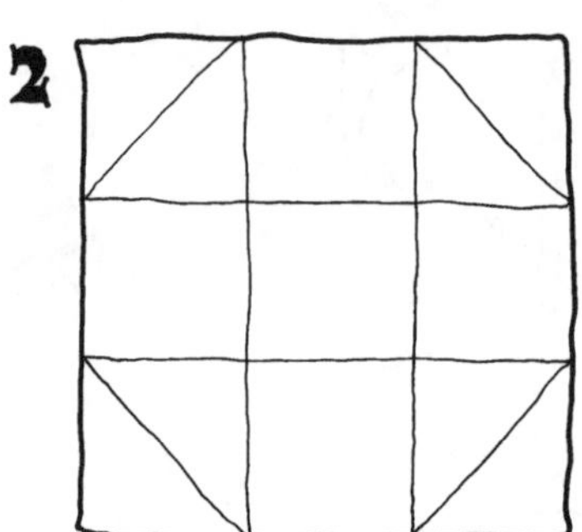

3

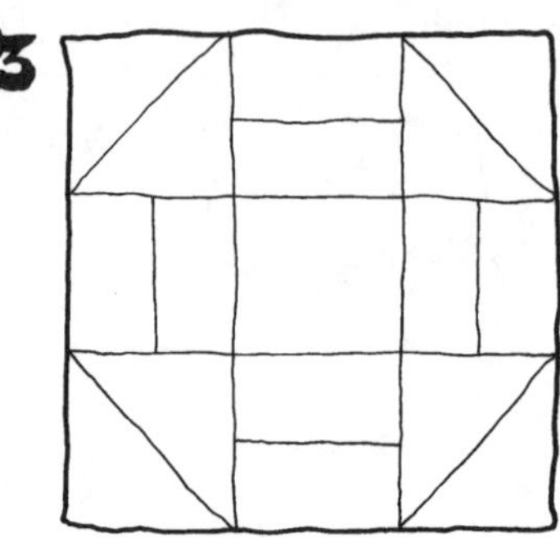

4

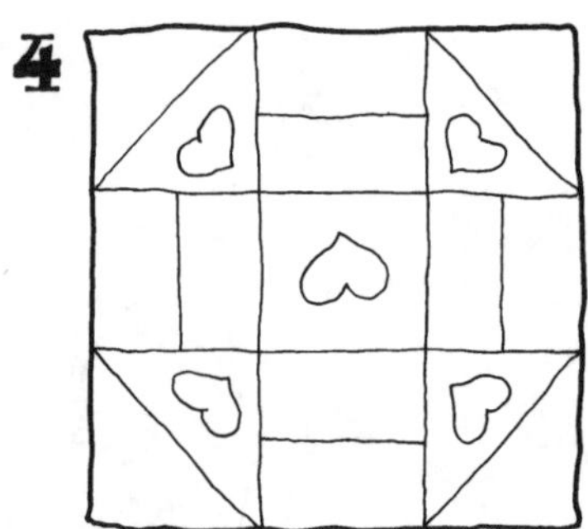

5

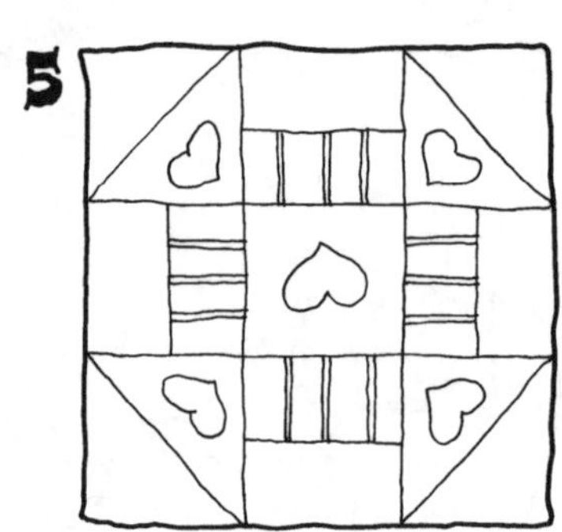

6

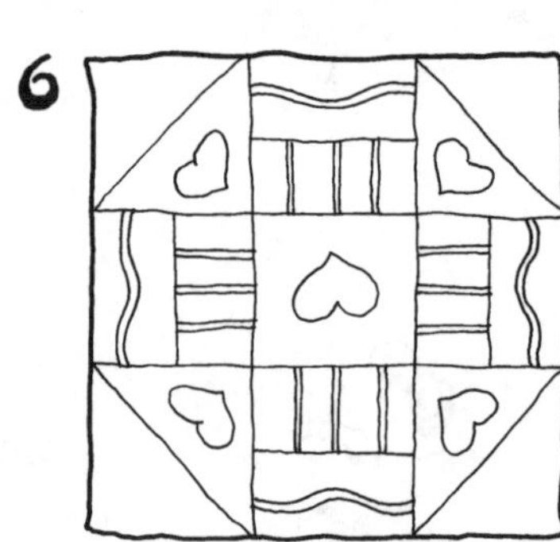

7

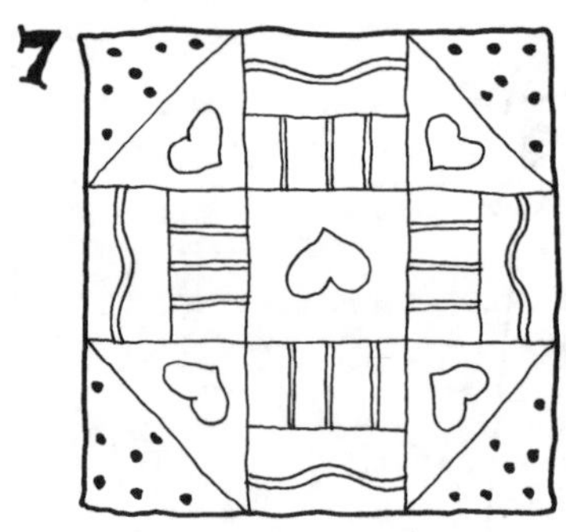

8

Our School

Answer sheet

Activity on page 38

1

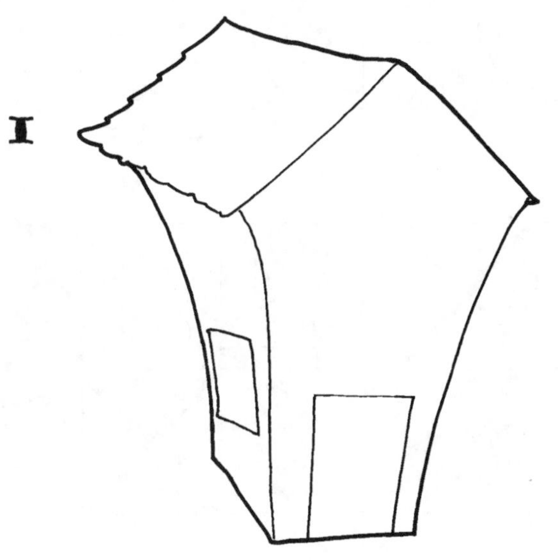

2

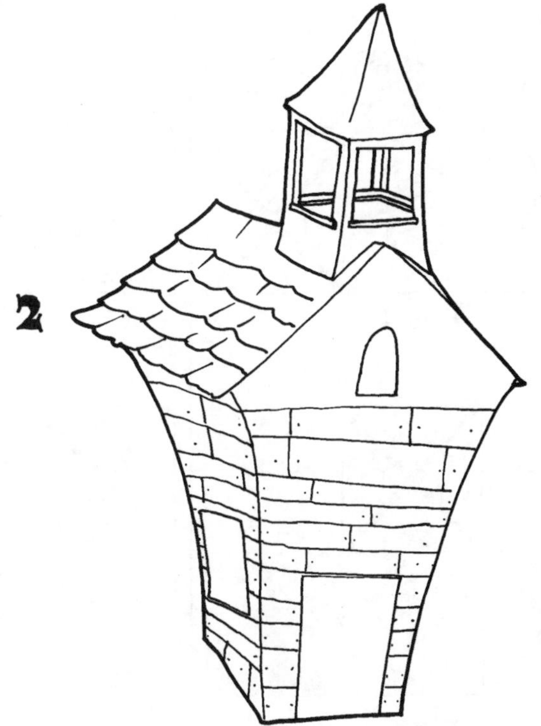

3

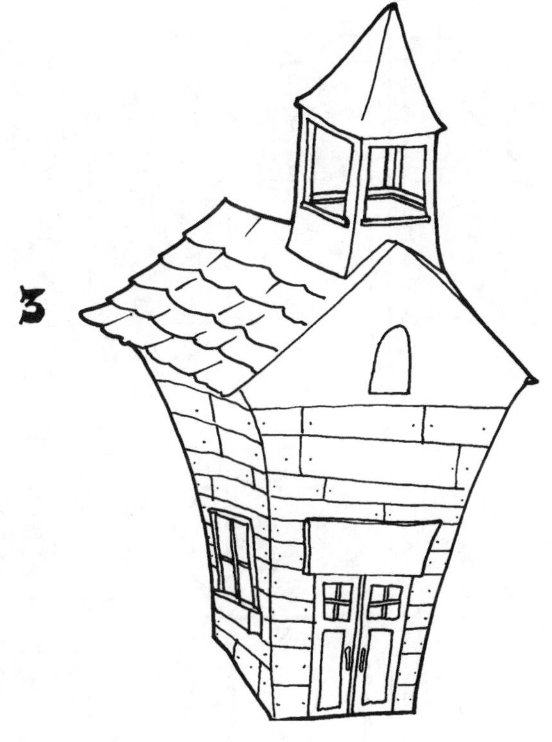

4

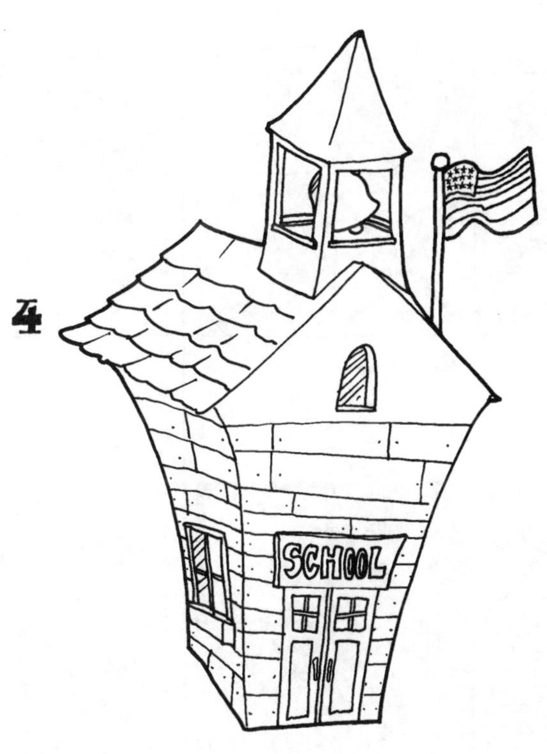

Answer sheet

Activity on page 108

Problem 1

Clue 1

Clue 2

Clue 3

Clue 4

Problem 2

Clue 1

Clue 2

Clue 3

Clue 4

Problem 3

Clue 1

Clue 2

Clue 3

Clue 4

Answer sheet

Activity on page 113

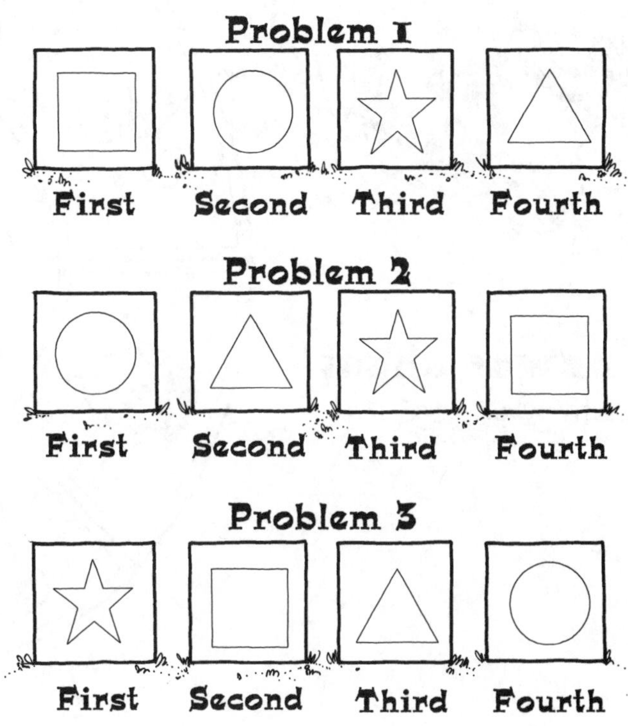

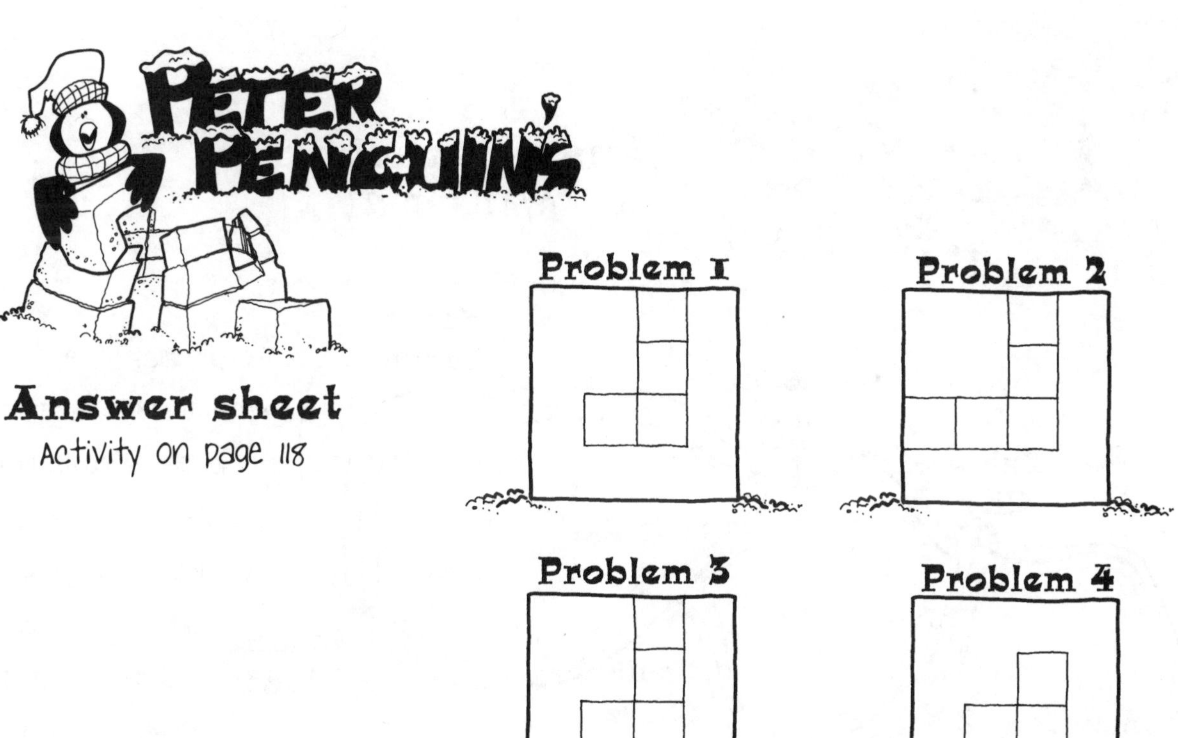

Answer sheet

Activity on page 118

Answer sheet
Activity on page 124

Kim
Kirsten
Ben
Franz
Kao
Heidi
Mary
Carlos

Answer sheet
Activity on page 127

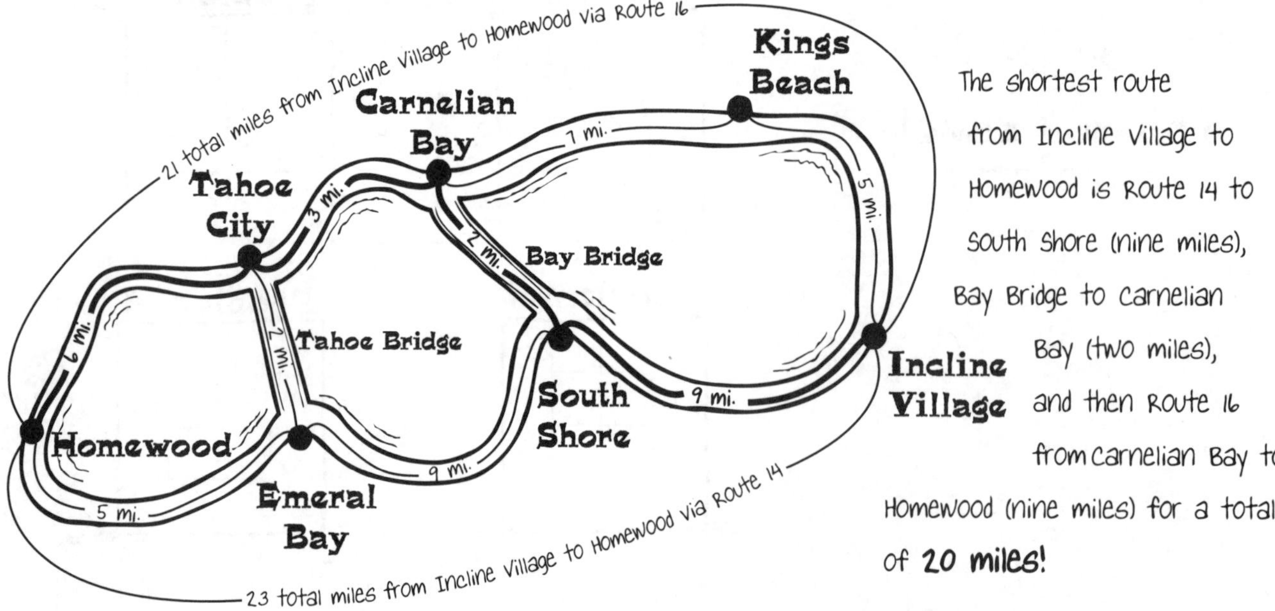

The shortest route from Incline Village to Homewood is Route 14 to South Shore (nine miles), Bay Bridge to Carnelian Bay (two miles), and then Route 16 from Carnelian Bay to Homewood (nine miles) for a total of **20 miles!**

historical MOMENTS

Answer sheet

Activity on page 129

1 **1593** Romeo & Juliet is published

2 **1767** Napoleon is born

3 **1795** Washington leaves presidency

4 **1797** Washington dies

5 **1837** Bicycle is invented

6 **1865** Civil War ends

7 **1866** Dynamite is invented

8 **1876** Telephone is invented

9 **1879** Lightbulb is invented

10 **1885** Rabies immunization is devised

11 **1963** "I Have A Dream" speech

12 **1964** MLK, Jr. wins Nobel Prize

13

14

15

16

17

Farmer John's Garden

Answer sheet

Activity on page 136

Shown below is one answer to each of Farmer John's Garden problems. Can you find other possible answers?

Problem 1

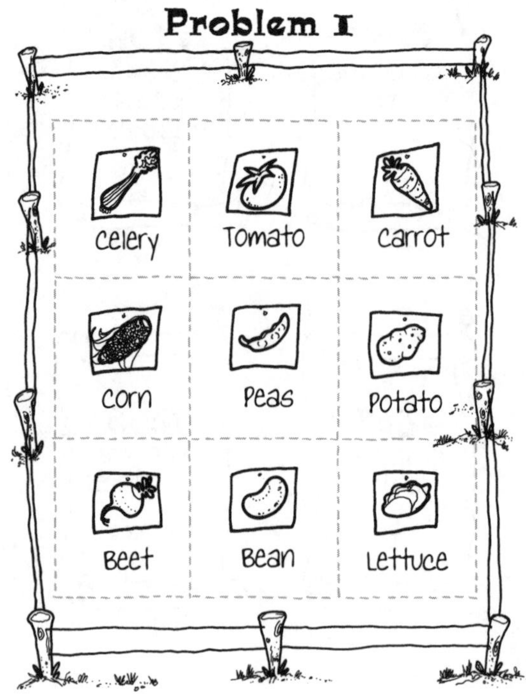

Problem 2

Problem 3

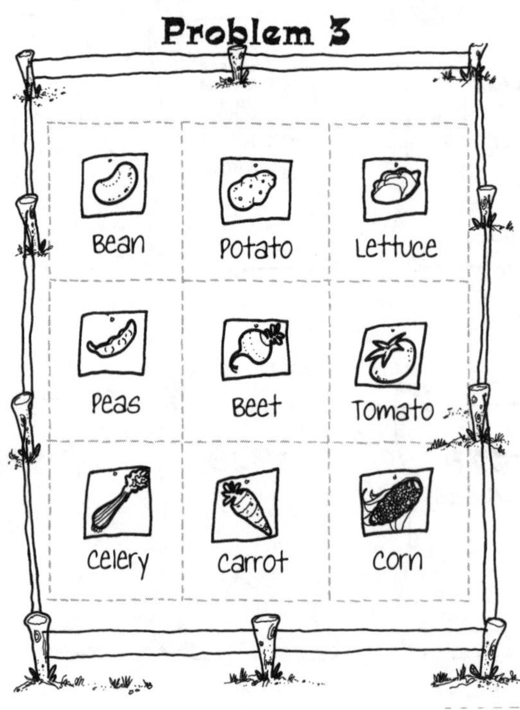

Barnyard Animals

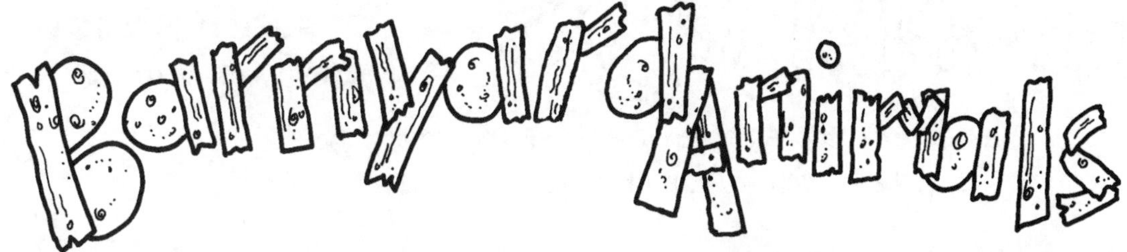

Answer sheet

Activity on page 142

Shown below is one answer to each of Barnyard Animals problems. Can you find other possible answers?

Problem 1

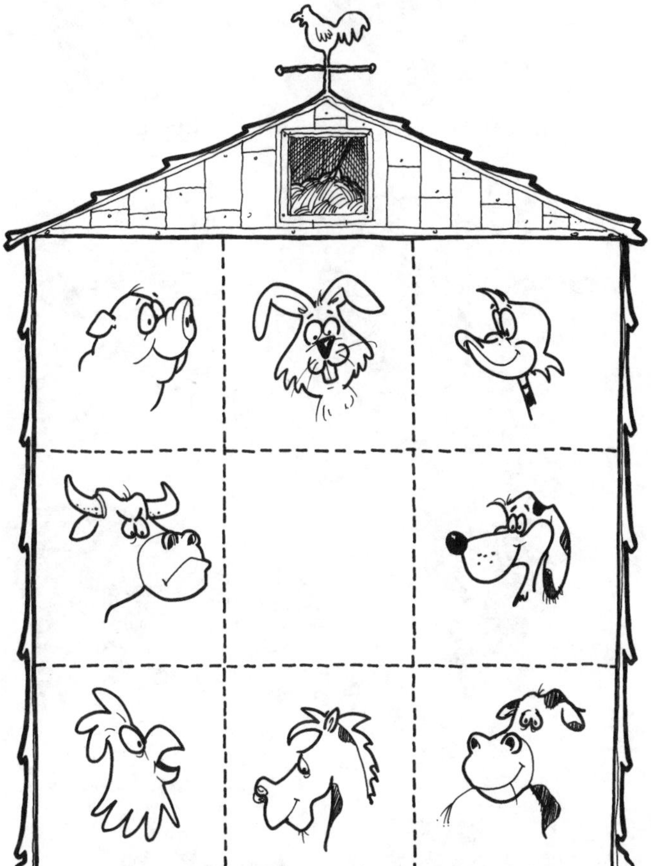

Problem 2

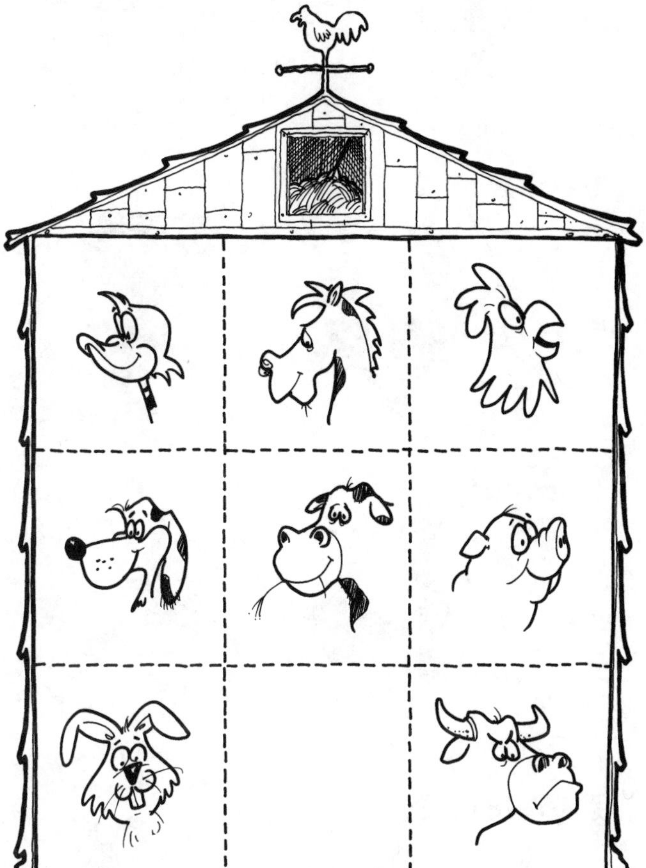

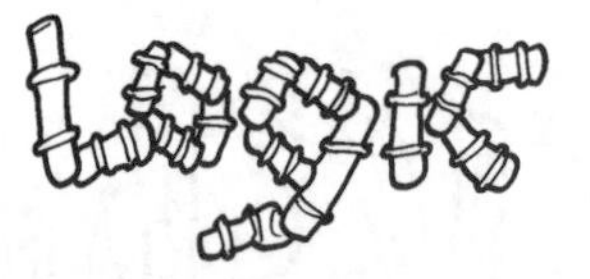

Answer sheet

Activity on page 148

Shown below is one answer to each of Rainforest Logic's problems. Can you find other possible answers?

Problem 1

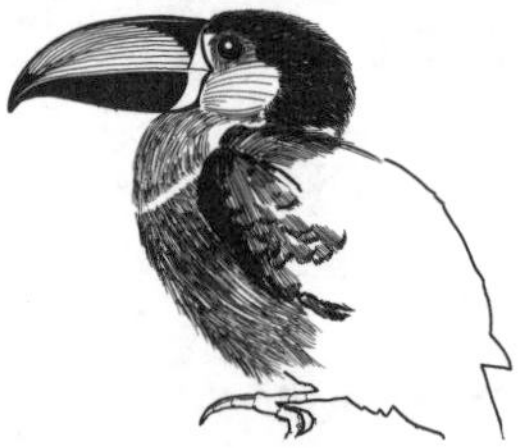

Toucan 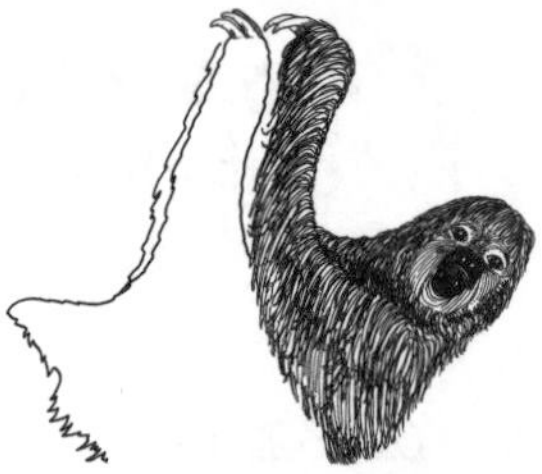 | Three-Toed Sloth 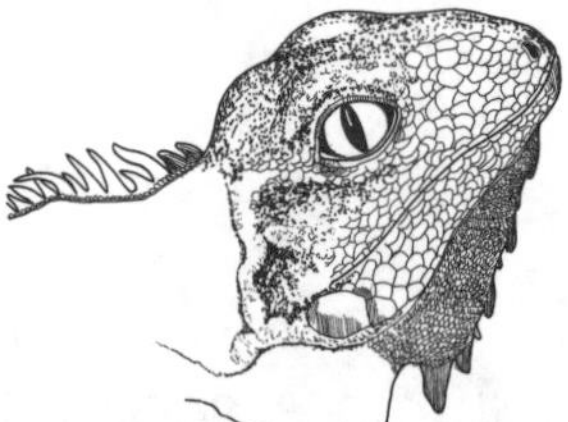 | Iguana 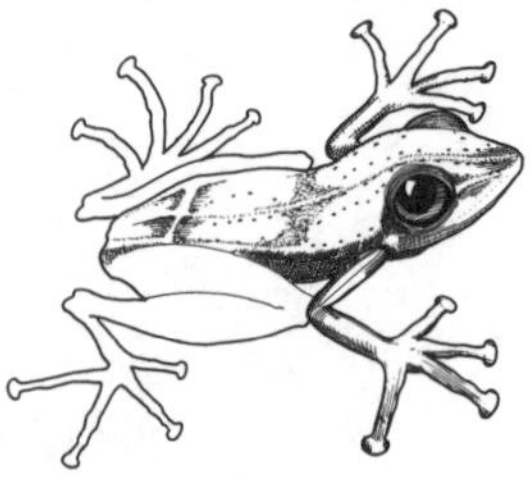 | Tree Frog

Problem 2

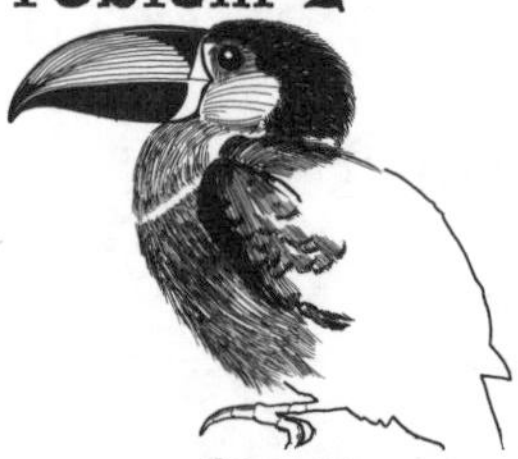

Toucan 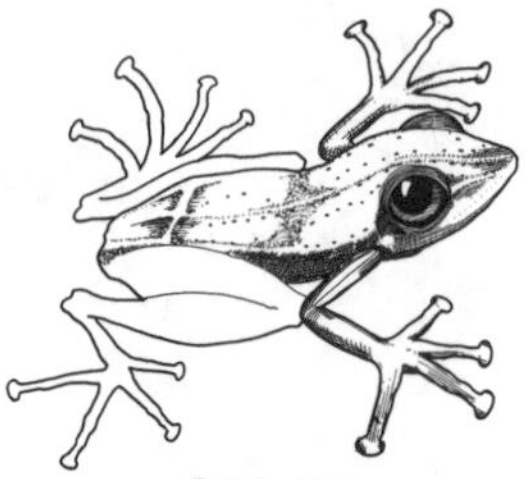 | Tree Frog 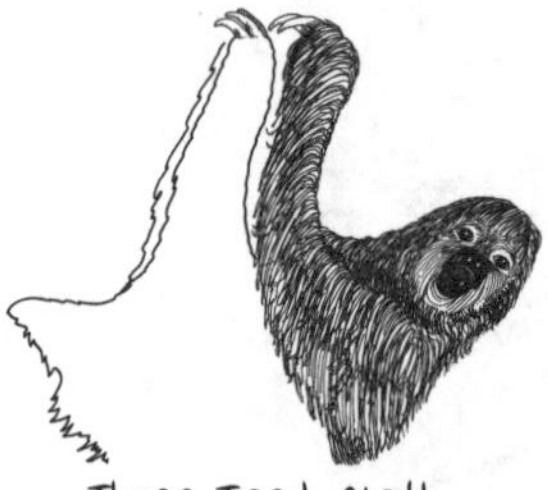 | Three-Toed Sloth 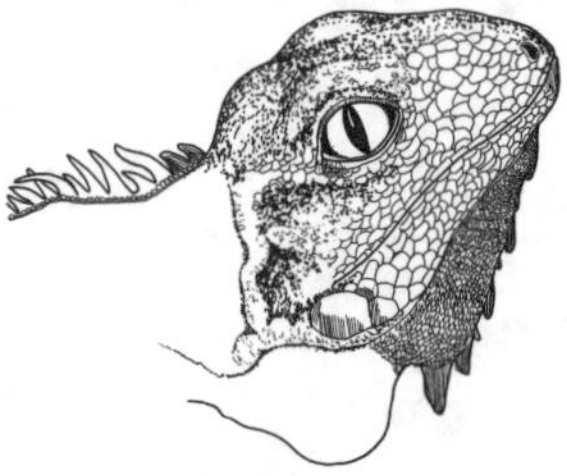 | Iguana

Problem 3

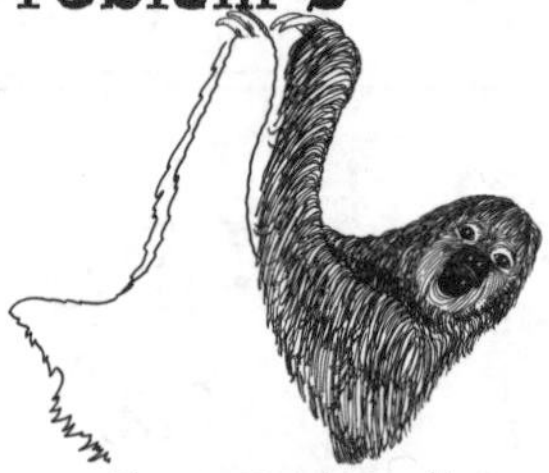

Three-Toed Sloth 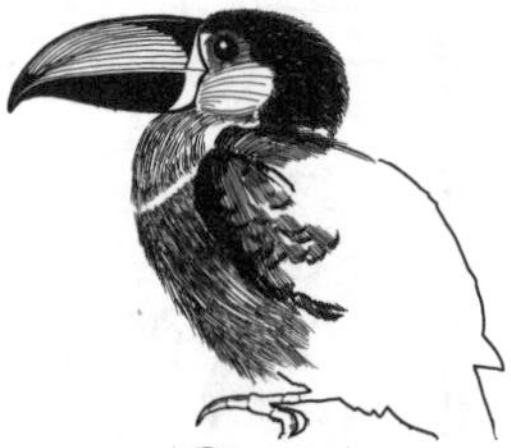 | Toucan 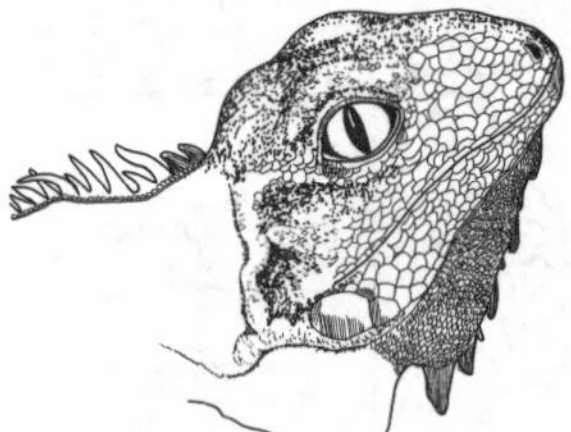 | Iguana 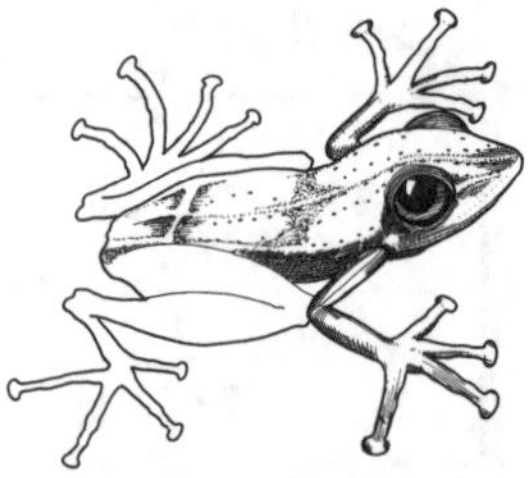 | Tree Frog

Problem 4

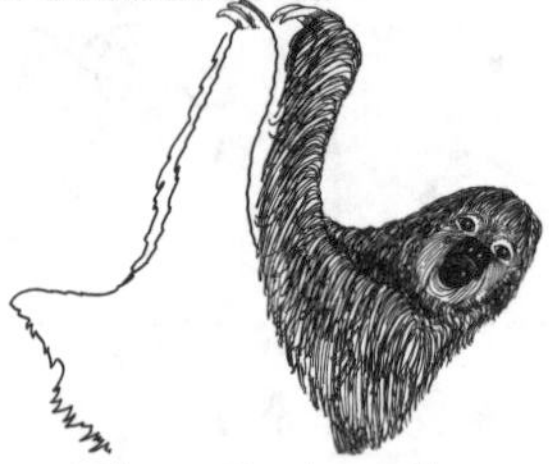

Three-Toed Sloth 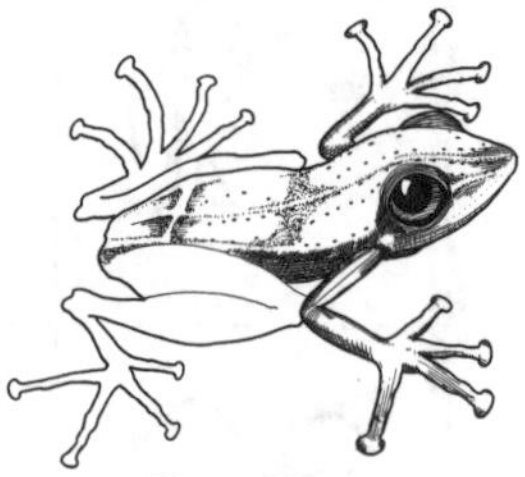 | Tree Frog 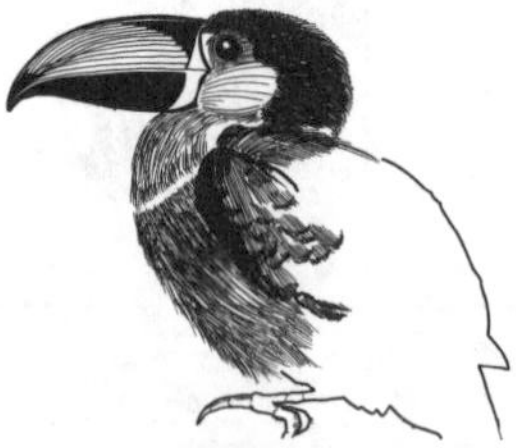 | Toucan 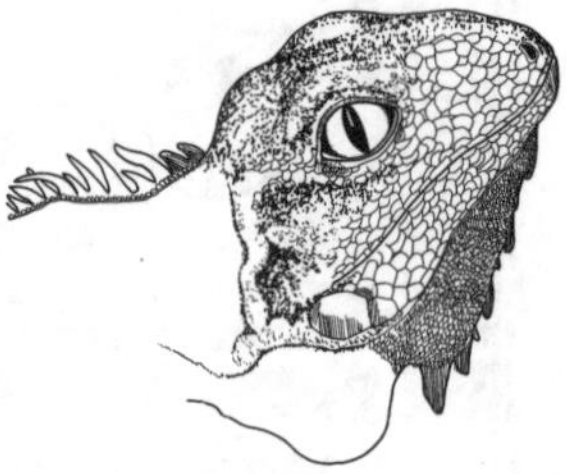 | Iguana

Problem 5

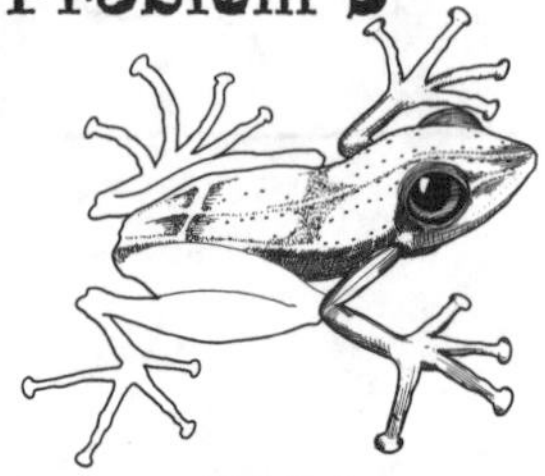

Tree Frog 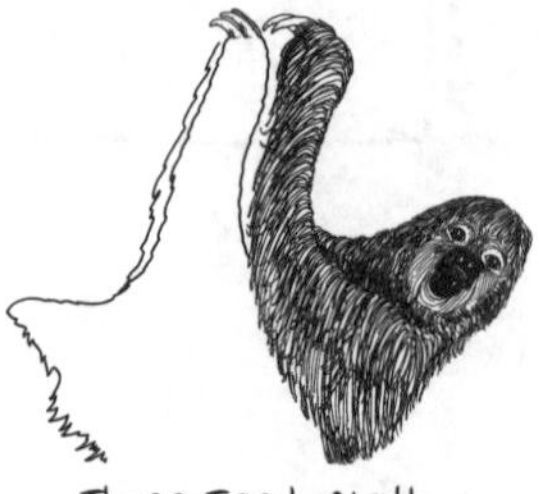 | Three-Toed Sloth 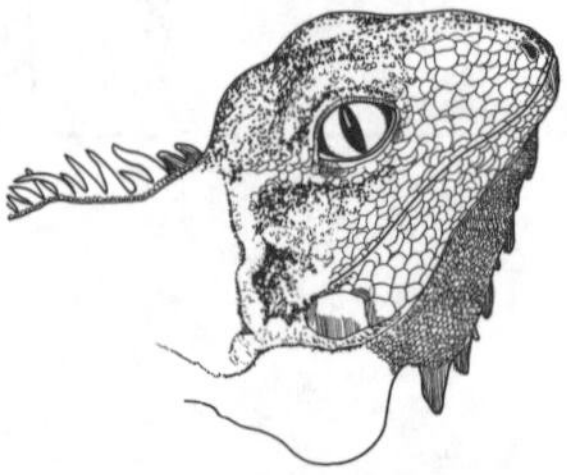 | Iguana 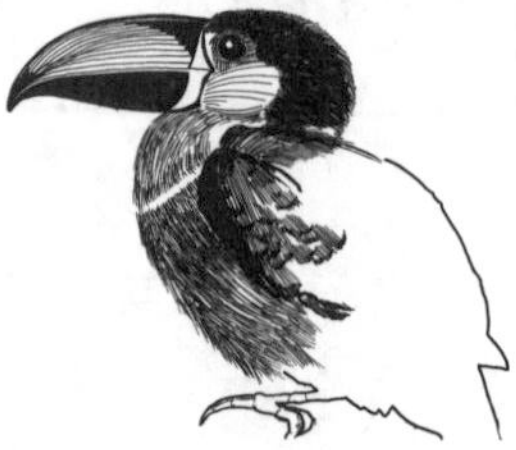 | Toucan

Answer Sheet

Activity on page 153

Shown below is one answer to each of Our Team's problems. Can you find other possible answers?

Problem 1

Joe – Least Letters; Toby; Maria; Patrick – Most Letters

Problem 2

Toby – Youngest; Joe; Patrick; Maria – Oldest

Problem 3

Patrick – Shortest; Maria; Toby; Joe – Tallest

Problem 4

Reverse order is ok

Patrick; Joe; Maria; Toby

Problem 5

Reverse order is ok

Maria; Patrick; Toby; Joe

Answer sheet Activity on page 158

Shown below is one answer to each of The Clown's Crayons problems. Can you find other possible answers?

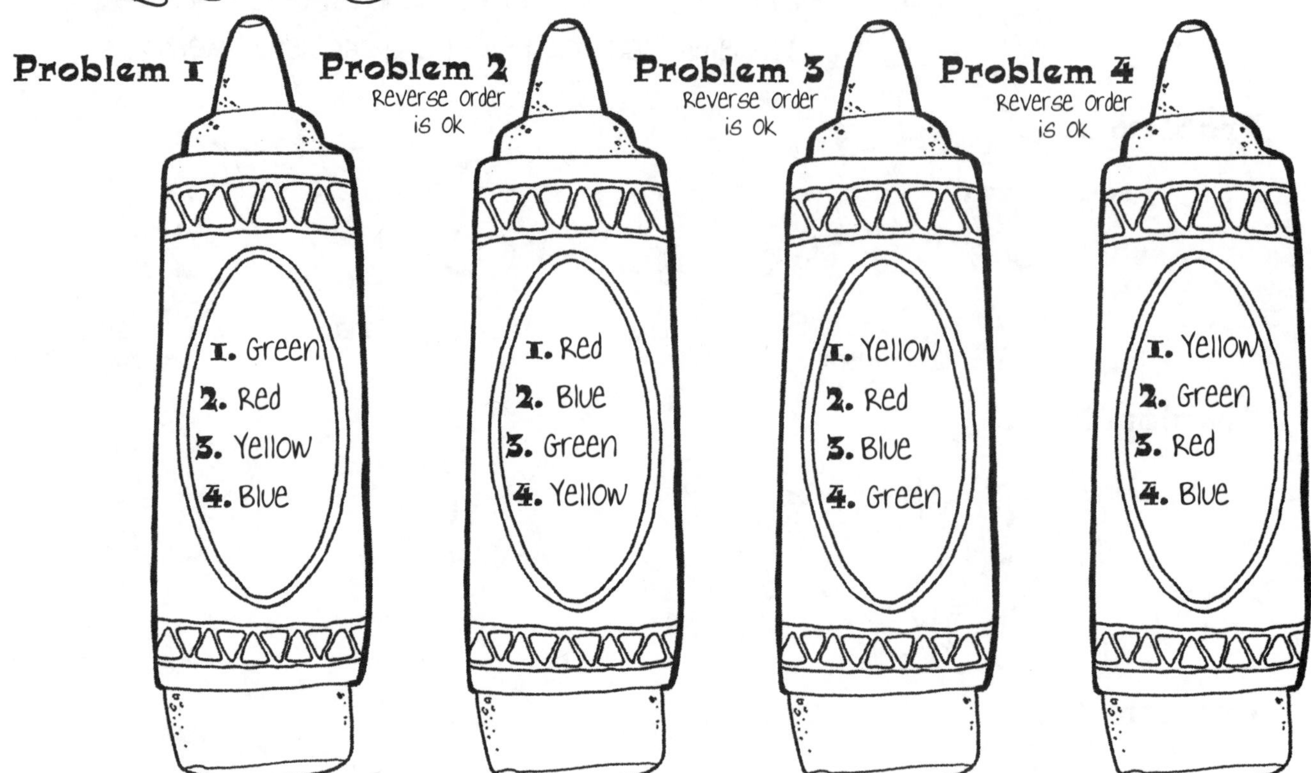

Pocket Change **Answer sheet** Activity on page 163

Shown below is one answer to each of Pocket Change's problems. Can you find other possible answers?

Answer sheet
Activity on page 168

Activity on page 168

Shown here is one answer each to problems one through four of Sunday Drive. Can you find other possible answers?

Problem 1

Problem 2

Problem 3

Problem 4

Answer Sheet

Shown here is one answer each to problems five through eight of Sunday Drive. Can you find other possible answers?

Problem 5

Driver

Problem 6

Driver

Problem 7

Driver

Problem 8

Driver

Answer Sheet

Activity on page 218

1. Striped fish direction
2. Tail of striped fish
3. Scales on tail of spotted fish
4. Air bubbles of spotted fish
5. Mouth of spotted fish
6. Pennant on castle
7. Castle turret
8. Window of castle
9. Seasnake position
10. Number of seaweed near castle
11. Crab eyelids
12. Belt buckle of diver's suit
13. Buttons of diver's suit
14. Diver's eyebrows
15. Scales of seahorse
16. Seahorse air bubbles
17. Number of stones in foreground
18. Points of crown
19. Treasure chest border
20. Pearl necklace on treasure chest

Answer Sheet

Activity on page 220

1. Window in door of bike shop
2. Sidewalk around gas pumps
3. Taco on snack shop sign
4. Number of coconuts in palm tree
5. Lion's tail
6. Tree in school yard
7. Roof of schoolhouse
8. Eagle on flag post
9. Stars on flag
10. Stripes on flag
11. Extra pennants in car sales lot
12. Missing pennants behind cars
13. Number on auto
14. The word "SALE" on truck window
15. Flower centers in central park
16. Extra car driving
17. Basketball court in park
18. Depth-of-pool; number of feet
19. Ladder in pool
20. Ball in pool

Answer Sheet

Activity on page 222

1. Spots on Big Dino
2. Tail on Big Dino
3. Teeth on Big Dino
4. Eyelashes on Big Dino
5. Volcano behind Big Dino
6. Number of spouting lava rocks from Big Volcano
7. Direction of flower, low right corner
8. Leaf of flower in foreground
9. Number of ants
10. Number of ant trails
11. Smile on Small Dino
12. Number of spines on Small Dino
13. End of tail on Small Dino
14. Claws on Small Dino
15. Number of palm trees
16. Number of flowers on lake plant
17. Front of Swimming Dino
18. Footprint color
19. Beak on Big Flying Dino
20. Second Flying Dino

Answer Sheet

Activity on page 224

1. Cereal popping in title
2. "Free" in bottom right corner
3. Belt Buckle
4. Stars on glove
5. Pattern on cereal bowl
6. Stripes on mask
7. Star on arm
8. Number of holes in belt
9. "Toy"/"T.V Show" on side of box
10. Stripe on side of box
11. UPC Bar code: 3 and 4 switch
12. Spoon on belt
13. Number of exclamation marks
14. "C" in title
15. "S" in "cereal" in title
16. Logo direction, top right corner
17. Bottom of box
18. "CC" on side of box
19. Link on necklace between "CC"
20. Razor stubble

Answer Sheet
Activity on page 226

1. Smoke from fireplace
2. Fireplace bricks
3. Bird on roof
4. Left side window
5. Person entering house
6. Baby in window
7. Flowerpot design
8. Steps to door
9. Mail slot
10. Door window
11. Horseshoe above door
12. Polka-Dot curtains
13. Flowerpot by chair
14. Flower pattern of chair
15. Chair frame color
16. Water faucet drip
17. Ladder
18. Ball coming out of window
19. Number of flowers in black pot
20. Shoelaces of person on ladder

The Train

Answer Sheet
Activity on page 228

1. Wheels on train
2. Train sign
3. Number of puffs of smoke
4. Stool position
5. Key position
6. Sign switch position
7. Cow position

Human Happenings Answer Sheet

Activity on page 232

Our early ancestors were hunters and gatherers. Cayonu textile, the oldest fabric ever found dates back to 8,000 B.C. Experts believe after this point, humans became more creative village farmers, and formed large-scale civilizations creating innovations such as the wheel, writing, and metal farming tools.

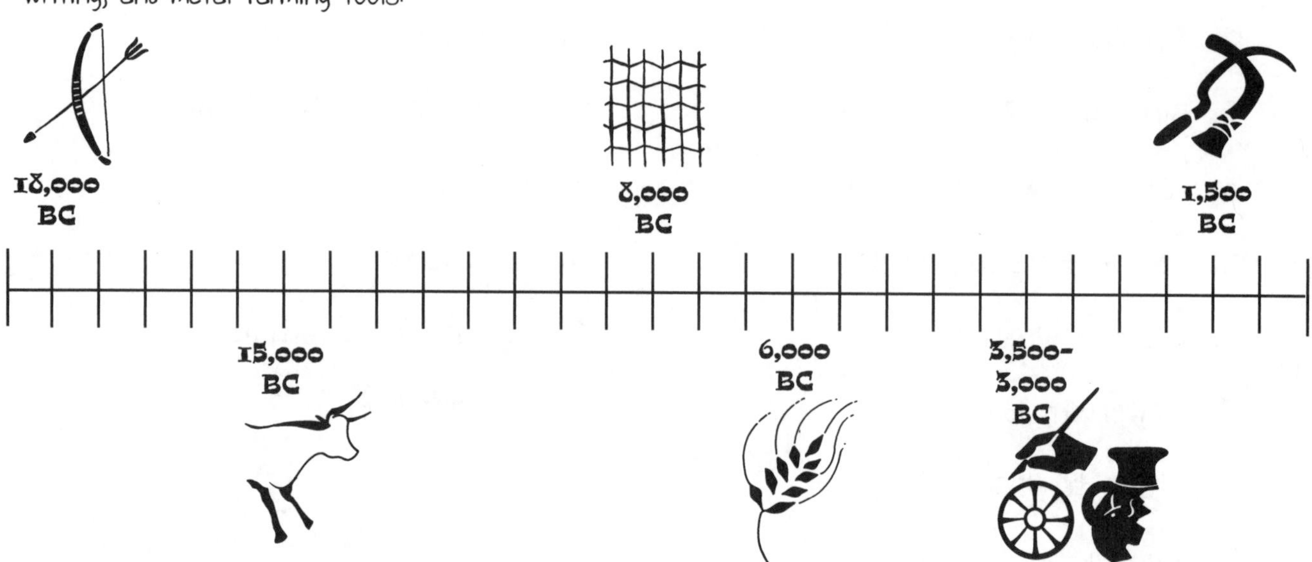

Answer Sheet

Activity on page 233

Shorty A. Tensionspan
2:55

Val U. Shopper
3:05

Ames High
3:25

Constance Whiner
3:40

Cher Leader
3:45

Neve R. Wrong
3:55

Lon G. Tude
4:10

Ima Winner
4:15

Mo Zart
4:20

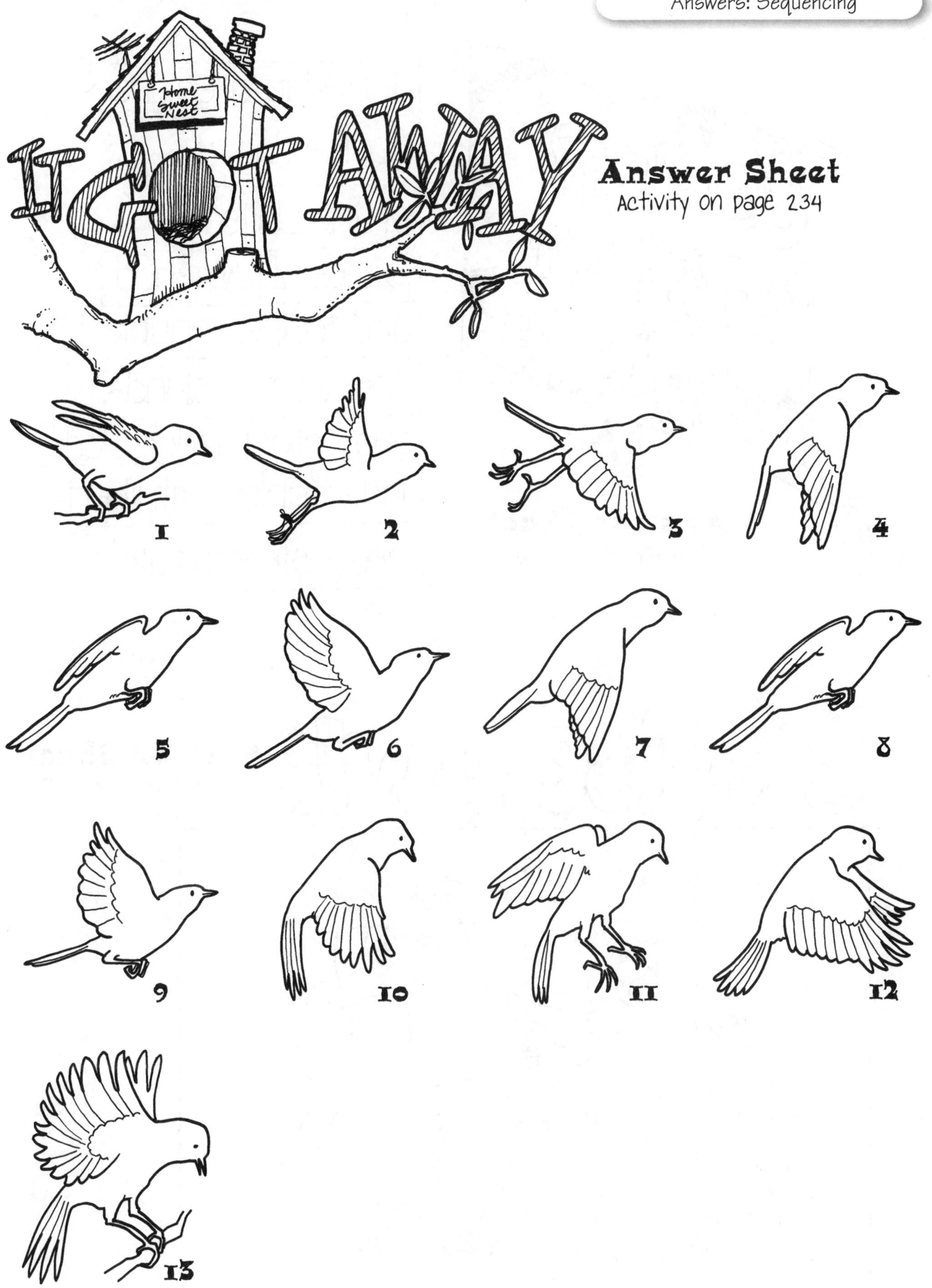

Answer Sheet

Activity on page 234

Answer Sheet
Activity on page 236

I pledge allegiance
to the flag
of the United
States of America
and to the republic
for which it stands
one nation under God
indivisable with liberty
and justice for all.

Answer Sheet
Activity on page 238

Answer Sheet
Activity on page 239

Maximum distance from sun	Diameter of planet	Length of day (Rotation time)	Length of year (Orbit time)
1. Mercury	1. Pluto	1. Jupiter	1. Mercury
2. Venus	2. Mercury	2. Saturn	2. Venus
3. Earth	3. Mars	3. Neptune	3. Earth
4. Mars	4. Venus	4. Uranus	4. Mars
5. Jupiter	5. Earth	5. Earth	5. Jupiter
6. Saturn	6. Neptune	6. Mars	6. Saturn
7. Uranus	7. Uranus	7. Pluto	7. Uranus
8. Neptune	8. Saturn	8. Venus	8. Neptune
9. Pluto	9. Jupiter	9. Mercury	9. Pluto

Answer Sheet
Activity on page 243

11:40
The Pig family decided to go to the beach.

11:40
The piglets were ready to leave.

11:45
Mrs. Pig was ready to leave.

12:30
Mr. Pig was finally ready to leave.

12:45
With the car packed, Mr. Pig lost his keys.

1:45
Mr. Pig found his car keys.

2:30
The Pig family were stopped as a train crossed.

2:55
The train passed.

3:02
Mr. Pig pulled into a rest stop for a bathroom break.

3:15
The policeman gave Mr. Pig a speeding ticket.

3:30
The Pig family arrived at the beach.

4:30
Mr. Pig returned with the food.

4:40
The piglets finished eating their food.

5:30
The piglet's food was finally digested.

MI Resources

Multiple Intelligences
The Complete MI Book

Dr. Spencer Kagan & Miguel Kagan (All Grades)

This new book is the single most comprehensive MI book available! If you're looking for one book on multiple intelligences—this is it! This resource guide will show you how to move beyond MI theory and make MI come alive in your classroom! Learn to match, stretch, and celebrate MI. When you match your instruction to how all students learn best, the classroom becomes more engaging for all learners with all patterns of intelligences. Reach students through their strengths. Prevent discipline problems stemming from disinterest. You'll accelerate learning and achievement, especially for "nontraditional" learners. As you stretch students' multiple intelligences, you develop students' many ways of being smart. Learn to easily stretch students' art, nature, space, music, body, people, and self smarts as well as their math and word smarts. Celebrate students' multiple intelligences in your classroom to make students feel valued and accepted for their own unique pattern of intelligences. Students will see themselves not as "weird" or "different," but smart in different ways. You will boost students' self-esteem and liking for school. You will promote a more positive, accepting classroom atmosphere in which students appreciate the differing patterns of intelligences of classmates. 720 pages. **BKMI**

"The single most comprehensive MI book available for teachers, teacher educators, staff developers, and administrators!"

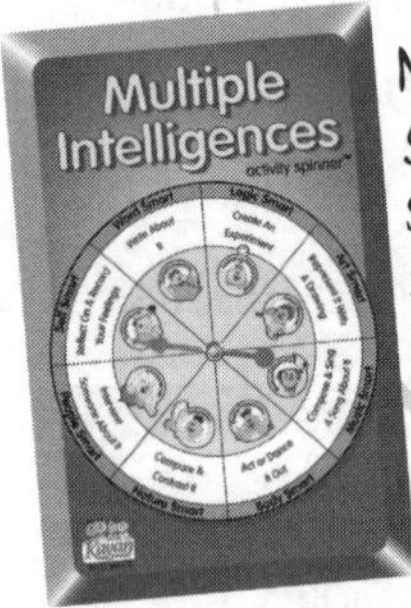

Multiple Intelligences Activity Spinner Combo Kit

Stretch your students' intelligences in many ways with the Multiple Intelligences Spinner! Use this little gem of a spinner to give your students many windows into any topic you're studying. Randomly select one of eight MI activities you can use with just about any learning topic. Includes dozens more alternative MI activity ideas on the back. Great for MI learning centers, MI team projects, or MI sponge activities. These involving activities will make your classroom burst with energy as you match, stretch, and celebrate your students' many ways of being smart! Combo includes eight spinners. **CMSMI** Individual Multiple Intelligences Activity Spinner **MSMI**

Multiple Intelligences SmartCard

This colorful 11" x 17" SmartCard is a terrific quick reference for multiple intelligences. It describes MI theory in a nutshell, describes the eight intelligences (including the naturalist intelligence) in plain, easy-to-understand language, and provides a long list of activities for you to do with your students to develop each of the eight intelligences. A great teacher reference to turn to time and time again. **TMI**

Multiple Intelligences Course Workbook

This is the perfect tool to lead participants through your MI class or training. A terrific companion workbook to The Complete MI Book for any training. Includes tabbed sections on the three MI visions for education; the eight intelligences; MI strategies, activities, lessons, projects and theme units; creating the MI class and school; and MI assessment. Workbook consists of note-taking pages, ready-to-use pull-out activities for your training, and blackline masters for participants to use with their students. 470 pages. **NMI**

Colorful MI Transparencies for Teachers and Trainers

Includes 86 vibrantly colored overheads to make your training come alive. An indispensable tool for MI teachers and trainers. Designed to lead participants through the complete MI course. Integrated with both The Complete MI Book and the MI Course Workbook. Includes sections on the MI visions, intelligences, instructional strategies, creating the MI class and school, and MI assessment. Colored transparencies are packaged in sheet protectors in an easy-access three-ring binder. **NMIT**

Multiple Intelligences Transparency Slideshow Binder

The perfect multiple intelligences training tool! Integrate the verbal, visual, and musical intelligences as you make multiple intelligences theory come alive for your participants. This binder makes introducing or reviewing MI easy —the slideshow virtually runs itself. Just dim the lights, put on soothing background music, take a seat by the overhead projector, and lead your participants through the MI show—a sequenced set of 35 colorful transparencies. Your participants will delight in the visuals, learn about the many facets of each intelligence, contemplate the insightful quotes, and chuckle at the humorous MI classroom cartoons. Let Kagan do the work for you. Your participants will love it! Make this proven, successful resource a part of your training. You may also use the individual transparencies separately as you train MI. 35 color transparencies. **NMITS**

Multiple Intelligences CD

Includes 30 tracks! Ten songs to celebrate the multiple intelligences, five bonus tracks from The Complete MI Book, and 15 music-only sing-along tracks. Celebrate MI through the musical intelligence! **LCDMI**

Multiple Intelligences Video

Part of Every Lesson

Dr. Spencer Kagan & Laurie Kagan

(All Grades)

In this video, Dr. Spencer Kagan and Laurie Kagan demonstrate how multiple intelligences can become an integral part of any lesson through easy-to-use MI strategies. After Dr. Kagan provides the theory, watch the eight intelligences come alive in eight classrooms as Laurie demonstrates a different MI strategy for each intelligence. An excellent video highlighting practical strategies to make classrooms come alive with usable MI strategies. **VMI**

Cooperative Learning & Multiple Intelligences Videos

Featuring Dr. Spencer Kagan & Laurie Kagan (Grades K-12)

The theory of multiple intelligences and cooperative learning form a powerful union resulting in more effective teaching and learning for all students. In this video, you will: discover how to teach all content areas through cooperative learning and multiple intelligences; explore instructional strategies for each of the multiple intelligences; observe demonstrations of many new cooperative learning and MI strategies; learn to provide successful learning opportunities for students of every intelligence profile; learn to teach with, for, and about all the intelligences—as part of any lesson. Each video program includes one videotape (approximately 50 minutes) and a soundtrack cassette tape. Elementary, **DVMIE;** Middle School, **DVMIM;** High School, **DVMIH;** Buy all three videos together and save. **DVMIC**

Notes

Notes

Notes